A1232820
3/77

W9-CCP-405

DEC 1 1992

DATE DUE

2 8 '82			
NOV 9 1992			

Ancient Peoples and Places

NORTHERN ITALY
BEFORE ROME

General Editor

DR GLYN DANIEL

ABOUT THE AUTHOR

Born in 1935, Lawrence Barfield studied in Cambridge under Grahame Clark and Glyn Daniel. After a short excursion into Chilean archaeology and a period of study in Jugoslavia, he devoted several years of research into the Neolithic of Northern Italy, where he has carried out a series of excavations, among others, on the key sites of Rivoli and Molino Casarotto, Fimon.

From 1961 to 1963 he was assistant to the professor of Prehistory in the University of Bonn and later (1963–64) carried out numerous excavations for the Rheinisches Landesmuseum in Bonn.

Since 1966 he has been lecturer in European Prehistory at the University of Birmingham, where he is also involved in local archaeological work as secretary of group 8 of the Council for British Archaeology.

NORTHERN ITALY

BEFORE ROME

Lawrence Barfield

73 PHOTOGRAPHS
69 LINE DRAWINGS
1 CHRONOLOGICAL TABLE
12 MAPS

WESTVIEW PRESS
1898 Flatiron Court
Boulder, Colorado 80301

THAMES AND HUDSON

THIS IS VOLUME SEVENTY-SIX IN THE SERIES

Ancient Peoples and Places

GENERAL EDITOR: DR GLYN DANIEL

First published 1971
© *Thames and Hudson Ltd 1971*
All Rights Reserved. No part of this publication
may be reproduced or transmitted in any form
or by any means, electronic or mechanical, including
photocopy, recording or any information storage and
retrieval system, without permission in writing from the publisher.
Filmset by Keyspools Ltd, Golborne, Lancs and
printed in Great Britain by Camelot Press Ltd, Southampton.
Not to be imported for sale into the U.S.A.
ISBN 0 500 02075 2

CONTENTS

LIST OF ILLUSTRATIONS

PLATES

FIGURES

Foreword

Throughout much of history and prehistory, the inhabitants of Northern Italy have looked northwards across the Alps, rather than to the Mediterranean world, for their political and cultural traditions. This orientation of culture is already clearly recognizable by the time of the Early Bronze Age and can be followed, through to the Iron Age and later, into periods of Celtic, Lombard, Hohenstaufen and finally Austrian domination. The great arc of the Alps to the north, as much as one would expect to the contrary, seems to have been a negligible barrier to communication and trade.

For the student of European prehistory therefore, the north of Italy must be a key area of research, since it is here that we so often find the meeting point of the Central European and the Mediterranean worlds.

Our knowledge of the many thousands of years of human settlement of Northern Italy before the Roman conquest has been culled almost exclusively from the earth by the archaeologist: only a few vignettes of the last pre-Roman inhabitants are recorded by classical writers. Some of the earliest references to the Po Plain are found in the early legends of Greece. The Voyage of the Argonauts, for example, included a journey up the marshy River Eridanus (the Po), an account which may be an echo of early Greek voyaging in the northern Adriatic. More fascinating is another legend concerning the daughters of the sun. These ladies, while weeping for their brother Phaëton, drowned in the Eridanus, were turned into black poplars and their tears became drops of amber. This story possibly contains an attempt to explain the source of Baltic amber, which was traded to Greece from the Bronze Age onwards, via Northern Italy.

The more factual historical records of later classical authors, such as Polybius, Livy, Pliny and others, contain objective, although sometimes conflicting descriptions of the Celts, Ligurians, Raeti, and other native populations of the North, and these accounts have been referred to in writing parts of the later chapters of this book.

I should like to acknowledge here the comments and help I have had in writing this book from many different people, including A. Ammerman, J. Closebrooks, V. Susco, G. Guerreschi, R. Lunz, R. Perini, and especially my friends in the Veneto: Professor A. Broglio, Dr A. Aspes and L. Fasani. My thanks are also due to Glyn Daniel at whose suggestion this book was first conceived.

L.B.

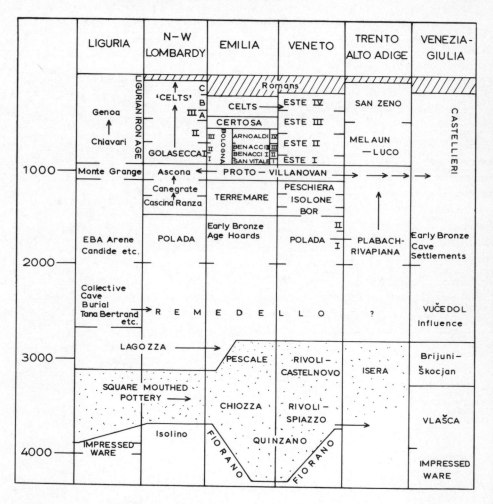

Chronological Chart

CHAPTER I

Introduction

THE STUDY OF PREHISTORY IN NORTHERN ITALY

Archaeologists first began to take a serious interest in the prehistory of Northern Italy in the middle of the nineteenth century, stimulated by discoveries elsewhere in Europe and in Etruria. Count Gozzadini's excavation of the Iron Age cemetery on his estate at Villanova, outside Bologna has a claim to be the earliest scientific archaeological excavation in the north. It was begun in 1855 and subsequently published (1855 and 1870). B. Gastaldi's slim volume of Italian Prehistory, mainly concerning Northern Italy, and entitled *Nuovi Cenni sugli Oggetti di Alta Antichita dell'Italia* was published in 1862. He discusses in this, among other things, the first Bronze Age finds from the *terremare* of Emilia and the peat bogs of the Southern Alps.

The remarkable antiquarian discoveries being made beyond the Alps inspired research into earlier periods of local prehistory. The excavations of Lartet and Christy in the caves of the Dordogne, for example, prompted A. Issel to take pick and shovel to the cave of Arene Candide in Liguria in 1864. Likewise, Ferdinand Keller's discoveries of Lake villages in Switzerland led the exiled French prehistorian G. de Mortillet, accompanied by two Italian enthusiasts, Stoppiani and Desor, to explore the lakes of Lombardy by boat. This voyage resulted in the discovery of the first Neolithic settlement at Isolino on Varese in 1863 as well as a whole series of other lake sites.

The final decades of the nineteenth century witnessed the activities of a remarkable generation of parttime prehistorians, whose output of excavation and publication was in some cases prodigious. A. Issel put Ligurian prehistory on the map, Pompeo Castelfranco brought to light and classified the Iron Age in Lombardy as well as pioneering other fields. A. Prosdocimi excavated innumerable tombs at Este in the Veneto and proposed his still valid fourfold chronology of the Este culture in 1882, while Zannoni, Gozzadini, Brizio, Montelius, Grenier and others rendered a similar service for the Emilian Iron Age through their studies of the large cemeteries at Bologna. G. Chierici carried out an impressive programme of research on the Neolithic period in Emilia from 1865 onwards while Scarabelli's publication of his excavation on the Bronze Age settlement at Monte Castellaccio (Imola) in 1887, is still an exemplary piece of work even by present-day standards.

At the turn of the century in Trieste, where work on local prehistory had been initiated by the British Consul and the ex-Orientalist, ex-explorer Richard Burton, G. Marchesetti continued research almost single-handed, and his voluminous publications of cave excavations at the great Iron Age cemeteries of Santa Lucia and the Istrian hill-forts *(castellieri)* are still the main sources for the prehistory of the Trieste area.

Field work apart, the International Congress of Prehistory in Bologna in 1871 and the founding of the *Bullettino di Paletnologia Italiana* in 1876 by the prehistorian from Parma, Luigi Pigorini, should also be mentioned, for both of these events proved to be catalysts for late nineteenth-century research.

This dynamic period of the study of prehistory had come to an end by the beginning of the First World War. Research thereafter tended to stagnate and only started picking up again shortly before the 1939/45 war, largely through the work of F. Malavolti and P. Laviosa Zambotti. Today much useful work is being done under the auspices of the national antiquities service in the different regions and by universities and local museums.

GEOGRAPHICAL BACKGROUND

The scope of this book is the area under present-day Italian political control which lies to the north of the Apennines and extends from Liguria in the west to the region of the Venezia Giulia in the east.

Fig. 1

The largest and most important geographical feature of this part of Italy is the vast flat and fertile Northern Plain, a roughly triangular expanse of alluvial deposits bounded by the Alps, Apennines and the Adriatic Sea. Its southern margin between Rimini and Turin measures some 260 miles while to the north the plain extends in an arm beyond Venice to take in the area known as Friuli at the head of the Adriatic. The width of the plain, which increases towards the east, is about 65 miles at Verona and its level surface is broken by only three main groups of hills, the Monferrato range in Piedmont and the small, but for the prehistorian important, Berici and Euganean Hills in the Veneto.

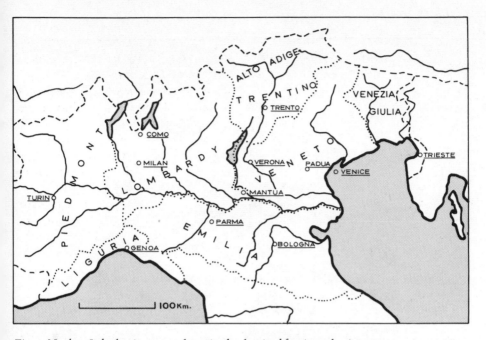

Fig. 1 Northern Italy showing present-day regional and national frontiers and main towns

Innumerable rivers descending from the surrounding mountains flow across the Plain either to add their waters to the great central axis of the Po or else, like the Adige and rivers beyond it to the east, to flow directly out into the Adriatic.

Although fertile, the Central Plain has never been a particularly pleasant place to live in. Before the construction of dykes and embankments, the flooding of large areas of the lower lying plain (bassa pianura) was an even commoner occurrence than it is today. The rivers too, including the Po itself, have in the past frequently left their beds to channel new courses, often with disastrous results. Ferrara and Este, for example, have since the Roman period been abandoned by the very rivers to which they owed their existence. In earlier times too, there were extensive tracts of noxious marshes extending from the Po delta up stream, and although the draining of these is said to have been started by the Etruscans, it is only in the last century that they have been finally brought under control.

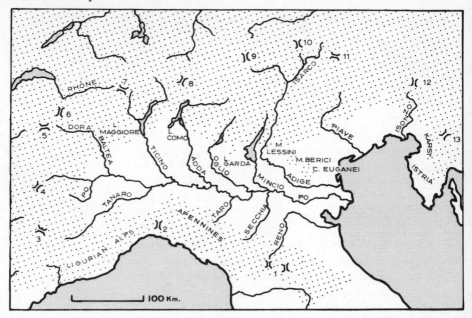

Fig. 2 Northern Italy and the Alps showing rivers, lakes, mountains and the main passes used in prehistoric times. The passes are numbered as follows : 1 Futa and Collina ; 2 Scoffera; 3 Col de l'Argentière; 4 Col du Mont Genevre; 5 Little St Bernard; 6 Great St Bernard; 7 Simplon; 8 San Bernardino (Mons Avium); 9 Reschen Scheideck (Passo di Resia); 10 Brenner; 11 Pustertal; 12 Predil; 13 Postojna. There is evidence to suggest that passes 1, 3, 6, 9 and 13 were in use by the end of the Neolithic period

These natural hazards deterred early settlement and the main concentrations of villages and towns have usually been along the margins of the Plain, skirting the Alps to the north and the Apennines to the south. Their proximity to the end of trade routes across the mountains was an added attraction for some of these peripheral settlements whilst others must have flourished on account of the presence of markets, where the produce of mountain and plain could be exchanged.

The rivers must always have been vital lines of communication and although it is difficult to find archaeological evidence for this, it is perhaps worth remembering that the earliest Roman colonial foundations in the central Po Valley, Cremona and Piacenza, in the first years of their existence relied for their survival on the river route to the Adriatic.

For the archaeologist the Po Plain presents some special problems. It has been calculated that the River Po carries some fifty million cubic yards of silt to the sea annually, and when in flood much of this is deposited on the land, resulting in the disappearance of many ancient sites beneath several feet of alluvium. The depth of this accumulation is also increased in some areas through localized geological subsidence (bradism). For these reasons Neolithic levels at S. Ilario (Emilia) lie at a depth of eighteen feet while at Russi, in the lower plain, Roman settlement remains lie no less than thirty-three feet deep. Normal archae-ological excavation of sites like these is virtually impossible and the likelihood of their being found at all is somewhat slender, dependent as it is on chance commercial exploitation of gravel or brick earth.

The Pleistocene glaciers of the Central Alps left an indelible mark on the northern fringe of the plain, gouging out the series of deep lake beds, which extended from Maggiore to Garda, and forming the characteristic hilly landscapes of gravel moraines south of these lakes. The great mass of water in some of the larger lakes, especially Maggiore and Garda, has even led to the creation of warmer microclimates around them, which, combined with the natural amenities of lakes as a source of food, greatly influenced the pattern of human settlement in these areas.

The North Italian Alps are penetrated by a number of spacious glacial valleys which attracted the early inhabitants of the Plain. The Adige valley in particular was especially densely inhabited as from Neolithic times, while in the rest of the Alpine region we can recognize a rapid growth in population after the start of the Bronze Age.

The Alps too were important on account of their mineral wealth. From the Palaeolithic through to the Middle Bronze Age flint was quarried in large quantities in the Lessini Mountains north of Verona, from the deposits which at a much later date were to supply Napoleon's armies with gun flints. Suitable hard greenstone rocks, which were used in the manufacture of axes in Neolithic times, are also to be found along the whole fringe of the Alps. Copper, silver and gold were all mined in the central stretch of the Southern Alps, following the introduction of metal technology.

Fig. 2

Many of the Alpine passes were well known to travellers and traders well before the arrival of the Romans and there is some evidence to show that the Great St Bernard, the Reschen Scheideck (Resia) and the Postojna passes were already in use by the end of the Neolithic period.

The Apennine range to the south is lower and narrower than the Alps and composed of quickly erodible Tertiary sedimentary rocks. Its valleys are steeper and less inviting to settlement than those of the Alps, but it is easier to cross and there are numerous routes from the Plain to its western side. Along this northern stretch of the Apennines the most important passes are the Passo dei Giovi from Piedmont into Liguria and the Futa pass connecting the Saveno valley and Emilia with Tuscany.

At the opposite extremities of our area of study are Liguria and the Venezia Giulia. The precipitous and mountainous Ligurian coast would seem to provide a rather inhospitable environment for early man. At the western end of this coastline there is, however, a series of fine limestone caves which provide good shelter and some of these, like the cave of Arene Candide, were repeatedly used by the prehistoric populations of the coast.

To the east, on the rather similar rugged limestone plateau of the Trieste Karst and in the Julian Alps, there are many more caves than in Liguria. The cultures which developed around Trieste, as we will see, tend to be more closely connected with the prehistoric sequence of Jugoslavia than that of Italy, and the Predil and Postojna passes served to link this region, at an early date, with the Central Danube Basin.

The modern political divisions of Northern Italy, the regions (*regioni*), which are used as areas of reference in this book comprise Liguria, Piedmont, Lombardy, Veneto, Trento-Alto Adige, Venezia Giulia and Emilia. It is interesting to remember that these regions are to a large extent based on the administrative areas established by the emperor Augustus, for these in turn reflected the political set-up of Pre-Roman times, themselves natural areas of human settlement. In fact some of these regions still bear the names of their prehistoric inhabitants, as in the case of Liguria (Liguri) and the Veneto (Veneti). The region of the Trento-Alto Adige, corresponding to the southern part of the Roman province of Raetia, derives its name from the indigenous population, the Raeti; while the Roman region of Histria, of which the territory of Trieste is now the northern remnant, is named after the tribe of the Histri.

For some unexplained, possibly political, motive the Romans avoided all reference to the Celtic inhabitants of the Plain when they named the other regions of the Po Valley. Emilia, which has retained its Roman name, was so called after the Roman consul Emilius Scaurus even though it had previously been occupied by the Boii and other Celtic tribes, while the modern region of Lombardy, also formerly in Celtic territory, corresponds roughly to what the Romans called Transpadana, the land across the Po.

CHAPTER II

The Early Hunters

Fig. 3

Man first settled in Northern Italy during the Pleistocene, a period of geological time which started some two million years ago and which is perhaps better known to the layman as the Ice Age. It is a period characterized by great fluctuations in temperature when phases of intense cold, Glaciations, alternated with phases of more mild climate, Inter-glacials. The Glaciations, which covered Northern Europe with ice sheets, caused the growth of glaciers all along the southern edge of the Alps, with especially large ones in the central part of the Alpine region. Excavating deep channels through the mountains like gargantuan bulldozers, these rivers of ice periodically turned the land to the north of the Po into a spectacular waste of ice and gravel, only to retreat and melt during the warmer interglacial periods.

Four major Glaciations, the Günz, Mindel, Riss and Würm, to name them in chronological order, have so far been clearly recognized in the Alps, and whilst there is some evidence to suggest the existence of still earlier cold phases, these, as yet, cannot be satisfactorily defined. The Glaciations were themselves not continuous, but were interrupted by short fluctuations of warmer climate called Interstadials. During the Würm Glaciation, for example, there were two Interstadials (Würm I/II and Würm II/III) to which we will be referring later.

Another side effect of these climatic changes was the dramatic rise and fall in sea level. When the ice melted during an inter-glacial period the volume of water released caused the sea level to rise, so that the low-lying Po Plain was flooded, and beach lines are recorded at least as far west as Imola. On the other hand, the glacial periods produced a drop in sea level whereby the area of the Plain was greatly increased. It has been estimated that during the Würm Glaciation the whole northern area of the Adriatic would have been dry land about as far south as Ancona.

THE LOWER PALAEOLITHIC

Although no actual skeletal remains have been found in Italy, the earliest Italians probably belonged to the low-browed, heavy-jowled, *Homo erectus* type of man, fragments of whose skull have been found in

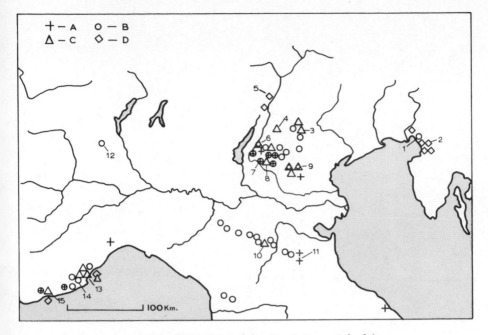

Fig. 3 Northern Italy with Palaeolithic and Mesolithic sites. A Lower Palaeolithic; B Mousterian; C Upper Palaeolithic; D Mesolithic sites; 1 Grotta Pocala; 2 Grotta Azzurra di Samartorza; 3 Riparo Battaglia; 4 Fiorentini; 5 Vatte di Zambana; 6 Ponte di Veia; 7 Quinzano; 8 Riparo Tagliente; 9 Grotta di Broion; 10 Savignano; 11 Correchio; 12 Ciaturun; 13 Arene Candide; 14 Toirano; 15 Grimaldi Caves

Pleistocene deposits at Swanscombe in England and Mauer in Germany. These people, who lived during the warm interstadials of the Riss glaciation and the following interglacial period did, however, leave a few of their stone tools along the fringe of the North Italian Plain.

The earliest datable find from the north so far, appears to be the rough flint hand-axe, of so called Abbevillian type, that was found deep down in a remarkable series of stratified deposits in the Cava Vecchia (the Old Quarry) at Quinzano near Verona. The level in which it was found can tentatively be dated to a warm interstadial phase of the Riss glaciation and the environmental evidence suggests that, in this area at this time, there was an open prairie landscape extending out from the Alpine

Fig. 4

Fig. 4 Quinzano (prov. Verona). Flint hand-axe of Abbevillian type. Lower Palaeolithic. (After Zorzi). 2 : 3

foothills, a grassland supporting herds of bison, red deer and the extinct great antlered deer, *Megaceros*, all of which would have been fruitful game for early man.

Higher up in the same Quinzano stratigraphy, flakes of Clactonian type, with obliquely-angled striking platforms, were found with a typologically more evolved kind of hand-axe (Acheulian), in deposits datable to the Riss-Würm Interglacial. Other hand-axes have been found at Lughezzano and Gazzo in the nearby Lessini Mountains. It is interesting that the Gazzo axe was found at a height of 541 feet, since all over Europe Lower Palaeolithic man normally kept to the lower plains and valleys and seldom ventured into mountainous terrain.

Finds of comparable antiquity have also been made in the area of Emilia. In the bank of the mountain torrent, the Correcchio, not far from Imola, tools and waste flakes were incorporated in a layer of sand and pebble which seems to have once formed an ancient shingle beach. Stratified immediately above this beach were sediment deposits such as would be laid down under a shallow sea. This geological sequence clearly relates to the rising sea level caused by the great melt at the start of the Riss-Würm Interglacial, when the whole eastern end of the Po

Plain lay beneath the Adriatic. These few tools are the last traces of a small group of hunters encamped on the sea shore during the final years of the Riss Glaciation.

The stone tools found at this site were similar to many of the surface finds found washed out of the gravels along the northern margin of the Apennines between the Rivers Reno and Santerno. These include primitive hand-axes of the Abbevillian type, finer ovate and pointed Acheulian hand-axes, and Clactonian waste flakes, mixed up with flakes of Levallois type, which were made by a more involved striking technique and are distinguished by their multi-facetted striking platforms. All these products were apparently manufactured at one period of time by the same group of people, suggesting that there is probably no chronological significance, at least in this area, in the typological difference between seemingly primitive Abbevillian and the better made Acheulian types of hand-axes. With no easily obtainable flint in Emilia, chert was usually employed in the manufacture of these tools.

THE MIDDLE PALAEOLITHIC

At the end of the Riss-Würm Interglacial and during the early centuries of the Würm Glaciation a radical transformation of culture is recognizable over the whole of Europe. A more varied and specialized selection of stone tools comes into use, and characterizes what the French prehistorian de Mortillet first called the Mousterian culture. This is the first manifestation of human culture in Europe which falls within the range of the carbon 14 method of dating. The dates of $44,450 \pm 1500$ and $38,650 \pm 1270$ BC from the Mousterian levels in the cave of Broion in the Berici Hills are closely comparable with dates obtained for this culture elsewhere in Europe. The thirty thousand years between 60,000 and 30,000 BC would seem to be a reasonable estimate for its span.

With the development of new technological ideas came also a new physical type of man, *Homo sapiens neanderthalis* or Neanderthal man. No certain skeletal remains of Neanderthal type have yet been discovered in Northern Italy, although several burials are known further south in the caves of Monte Circeo and Saccopastore near Rome. The nearest that we get to the physical remains of these people in the North are broad and flat footprints, belonging to at least two individuals, impressed in the wet clay of the floor of a cave, the Grotta della Basura at

Plate 2

Toirano (Liguria). Although these were not associated with any Mousterian tools, the fact that the cave entrance was sealed by ancient rock falls and that, together with the footprints, was the imprint of cave/bear paws, an animal extinct since the Middle Palaeolithic period, attests their antiquity.

Many more Mousterian than Lower Palaeolithic sites have been found in the North, and this may be due to the habit of the Neanderthalers, in contrast to their predecessors, of living in caves, where settlement deposits are well preserved. Neanderthal man was the first human being to adapt himself to the rigours of the glacial climate by means of efficient skin and fur clothing. He also foraged deep into the mountains, away from the well watered plains which were the haunts of *Homo erectus*.

Cave and surface sites producing Mousterian stone tools are known from the foothills bordering both the northern and southern margins of the Po Plain as well as from the sea/carved Grimaldi caves on the Franco/Italian frontier near Nice and from the Pocala cave north of Trieste to the east.

Mousterian tools were manufactured on flakes of flint and mainly consist of distinct varieties of points and scrapers. This basic tool/kit takes the form of a number of standard variations, and Palaeolithic specialists are not in agreement as to how far these different sorts of Mousterian culture reflect chronological, regional, or purely functional variations within the Mousterian tradition. However, it is worth noting that most of the sub/cultures represented in Northern Italy have almost exact counterparts in the Dordogne region of France and the differences can,

in the main, best be interpreted in terms of a chronological development in technology.

One variant of this Mousterian culture which seems to be chronologically the earliest, both in France and in Northern Italy, is that in which a large proportion of the flakes were manufactured by the Levallois method of flaking that we have already seen in the Lower Palaeolithic. In this method the cores and their striking platforms, from which the flakes were to be struck, were carefully prepared before the flakes were detached.

Fig. 5, c–e

This Levallois-Mousterian variant is represented in a level in the same deep stratified gravel quarry, the Cava Vecchia, at Quinzano (Verona) which produced the Lower Palaeolithic finds. It was here associated with the bones of elephant and fallow deer and the traces of a vegetation coverage which included abundant oak and laurel forests. This type of environment, according to Mr and Mrs Pasa, shows that the Riss-Würm Interglacial had not yet come to an end.

Slightly later in date must be the Levallois-Mousterian deposits in the two rock shelters of Mezzena and Zampieri in the Lessini Mountains, not far from Quinzano. Evidence for a later date is provided by the cold-climate cave bear and marmot which now occur, indicating that the first cold spell of the Würm Glaciation had set in. It is probably no coincidence that the earliest traces of hearths in the prehistory of Northern Italy were found in the levels of this period at the Abri Mezzena.

Similar Levallois-Mousterian deposits are known from the basal layers of the Broion cave in the Berici Hills, whose deep stratigraphy preserves

Fig. 5   Mousterian flake implements. a, b Grotta di Broion: points of la Quina type; c–e Emilia: scrapers and point of Levallois-Mousterian type. Note prepared striking platform and flake scars distinctive of the Levallois flake; f, g Grotta San Bernardino (Veneto) side-scraper with 'La Quina' step-flaking and denticulate flake scraper. (a, b after Broglio; c–e after Vaufrey; f, g after Leonardi and Broglio). a, b 2 : 3; c–e 1 : 2

an almost uninterrupted record of the development of environment during the whole course of the Würm Glaciation.

The Levallois-Mousterian is represented as well in surface sites in Emilia where, again owing to the local absence of flint, tools were still made from local coarse-grained rocks such as quarzite and chert. On the Ligurian coast a similar industry has been found in the Barma Grande cave (Grimaldi) and in the Grotta della Madonna near Taggia.

The finest products of the Mousterian culture are associated with the later so-called La Quina sub-group, which is also well known in *Fig. 5, a, b* France. Very finely made points and step-like retouch are especially characteristic of this development. The only pure assemblage of this particular group in Northern Italy is again from the Cava Vecchia at Quinzano, where a characteristic assemblage was found statified above the more archaic Levallois-Mousterian in deposits which show signs of having been formed when cold steppe conditions of the first cold period of the Würm Glaciation prevailed on the Plain.

Yet another variant of the Mousterian tradition, again with a French counterpart, was associated with hearths in the San Bernardino cave in *Fig. 5, f, g* the Berici Hills. Here, together with La Quina implements, there was a predominance of rather roughly made tools with jagged, or 'denticulate' edges, which gives this group the name of Denticulate Mousterian. The upper levels in this cave show every evidence of belonging to a fairly advanced stage of Mousterian culture, for not only does the fauna reflect the arrival of the warmer forest conditions of the first Würm Interstadial (Würm I/II) but new tool types, too, such as graving tools or burins, nose-scrapers and awls, presage the more advanced technology of the ensuing Upper Palaeolithic cultures.

Yet another variation on the Mousterian theme, the Alpine Mousterian, is represented in a number of caves along the arc of the Alps, from the Pocala cave near Trieste in the east, to the cave of Ciatarun near Borgosesia in Piedmont to the west, as well as in a few outlying caves in the Apennines to the south. One justification for singling out these sites as a distinct group is based on their location, often deep in the mountains. They are also distinctive in that they had geared their economy to hunting one species of animal, the cave bear. Their stone industry is usually of poor quality, with denticulate and Levallois techniques represented. The distribution of these cave-bear hunters extends beyond the Italian frontier into the alpine regions of France, Switzerland, Austria and northern Jugoslavia, where besides the specialized bear-hunting there is also some evidence that a cult was practised involving the hoarding of bear bones and skulls.

Neanderthal man, for all his rugged features, had a brain capacity not much different from our own. He was an innovator not only in the field of technology but also in man's spiritual development for, besides practising a cult involving bears, he was the first human to bury his dead in graves and cemeteries like those in the caves south of Rome. With him human progress had taken an important step forward.

EARLY UPPER PALAEOLITHIC CULTURES

Just over 30,000 years ago the technique of making long parallel-sided blades of flint was developed and prehistoric flint-workers turned to producing an enriched range of knives, borers and scrapers, and other tools manufactured almost exclusively on such blades. This technological revolution again appears to coincide closely with the appearance of a new human type, *Homo Sapiens Sapiens*, who differed from modern man only in his material culture. From now on man's cultural evolution forges ahead with ever greater momentum and variety.

In Northern Italy, Upper Palaeolithic remains are found only in caves of the Ligurian coast and the mountains fringes of the Veneto. In these two areas, however, we find stratified cave deposits which give us a reasonably uninterrupted story of the cultural development.

The flint industries of the Italian Upper Palaeolithic, even though they bear names derived from the roughly contemporary cultures of south-western France, developed independently of their French namesakes and there now appeared for the first time, all over Europe, a variety of regional cultures hitherto unknown.

Only at the most westerly extremity of the Ligurian coast do we find a development which in part closely follows the classic sequence of south-western France. Here the oldest finds of this period come from the level G in the Riparo Mochi and comprise tools distinctive of the Chatelperronian and the following Aurignacian phases. The overlying level F also contained a typical Aurignacian assemblage.

These Aurignacian people of the Ligurian coast hunted horse, cattle, deer and pig, all animals which are adapted to a mild climate, suggesting that the first warm interstadial phase of the Wurm Glaciation had not yet come to a close. The Aurignacian culture has not yet been identified elsewhere in the North although in Italy it also spread down the Tyrrhenian coast as far south as Sicily.

In the Veneto there is a possible indication of Chatelperronian influence in the Grotta del Mondo and the Grotta A at the Ponte di Veia, both in the Lessini Mountains. The Ponte di Veia is a spectacular landmark consisting of a natural bridge of limestone, formed by the mouth of a vast cavern whose inner roof had fallen in at some remote period of the Pleistocene. The smaller caves which cluster round this geological curiosity were used as shelters during the Upper Palaeolithic.

Plate 5

These earliest and poorly documented blade-tool industries were superseded by a uniform tradition of flint implement production in which small backed bladelets and points are the most distinctive artifacts. These are the hallmarks of the longest surviving and most widespread technological tradition of the European Upper Palaeolithic, the Gravettian culture, which is to be found from the Atlantic to Siberia and southwards into Italy and Greece. Although in France the Gravettian represents a relatively short episode in the Upper Palaeolithic, in Italy this tradition survives, in the form of the Epi-Gravettian, well into Post-Glacial times.

Following Broglio and Laplace, it seems possible to distinguish three main phases in the development of the Gravettian and Epi-Gravettian in Northern Italy. The earliest, called simply Gravettian, can be roughly correlated with the French Gravettian dating to the period between approximately the twenty-eighth and twenty-second millennia B C. The second and third phases, the Early Epi-Gravettian and Evolved Epi-Gravettian, occupy the period up to the end of the Ice Age when in France the Gravettian had been replaced by other cultures such as the Solutrean and Magdalenian which are not represented in Italy. A fourth phase, the Final Epi-Gravettian, belongs to the warmer times of the post-glacial period which starts about 8000 B C.

GRAVETTIAN AND THE EARLY AND EVOLVED EPI-GRAVETTIAN

The first of these phases, the Gravettian, is so far only known from the Grotta dei Fanciulli, level I-C and Riparo Mochi in the Grimaldi cave group. The presence of reindeer bones in the Grotta dei Fanciulli suggests that this deposit dates to the second cold phase of the Würm Glaciation (Würm II), while fauna indicative of a warmer period, the Würm II/III interstadial in all probability, was found with the Gravettian industry in the Riparo Mochi. It is interesting to note too that reindeer did not penetrate further into Italy than western Liguria since the arc of the Alps was an inpenetrable barrier for these and other cold climate animals of the northern Plains, such as the mammoth.

The flint artifacts of this early phase closely resemble the contemporary French Gravettian products, with large numbers of small backed points, end-scrapers and burins. The burins, or gravers as some prehistorians prefer to call them, include a very distinctive French type, the Noailles burin, which has a graving spall limited in length by a notch on the side of the blade.

A double burial of a mother and son was found accompanied by pierced sea shell ornaments in the Gravettian levels of the Grotta dei Fanciulli. For a long time these two skeletons had some notoriety, since it was claimed that they had negroid features and represented a group of African origin. This view however is no longer generally accepted.

The Gravettians were the first sculptors in the history of human art and the little figures of fat ladies with large buttocks and breasts carved in bone or stone are distributed over a large area of Europe. No less than fifteen small steatite figurines of this type were recovered from the Barma Grande cave at Grimaldi during the nineteenth century, while an extremely fine steatopygous figure of a woman carved in stone was found at Savignano in Emilia. However, although the Savignano figure belongs typologically to the Gravettian series of statuettes, it is curious that this is the only Gravettian find of any kind from the whole of Emilia.

The ensuing Epi-Gravettian stages are represented by a much larger number of sites, which like the other Upper Palaeolithic remains are restricted to the Ligurian coast and the Alpine foothills of the Veneto.

The Early Epi-Gravettian stage is found in the Grotta delle Arene Candide as well as in level C of the Riparo Mochi at Grimaldi, while the principal deposits of this material in the Veneto come from cave C at Ponte di Veja, Sala Grande in the cave of Broion, and the caves of Paina and Trene.

Two distinctive projectile points can be used as 'type fossils' for this period in the Veneto. One is a pressure-flaked point (*punta a faccia piana*)

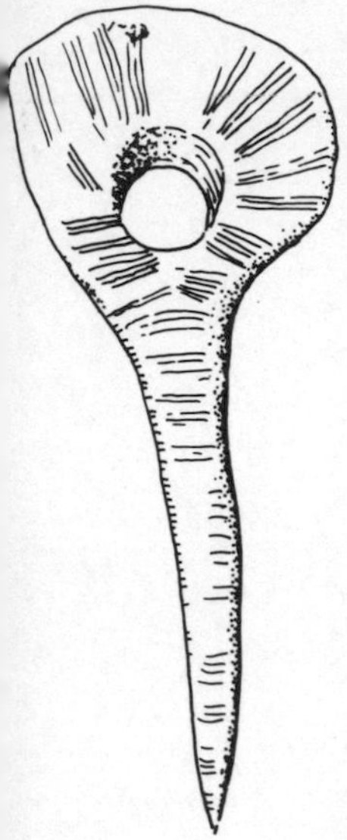

Fig. 6   *Arene Candide (Liguria).* Baton de commandement *(after Graziozi)*

perhaps related to the French Solutrean projectiles and the other is a shouldered point. Commoner flint tools from Epi-Gravettian sites are the small 'Gravette' backed points and angle burins, while sub-circular and discoid scrapers are a new and increasingly popular tool type. These people also made simple bone points, and continued to use sea shells – chiefly *nassa* and *columbella* – for ornaments. Pendants made from the incisor teeth of deer, which are widely distributed in European Upper Palaeolithic cultures and which are probably connected with some form of hunting magic, have been found in Early Epi-Gravettian levels in Grotta Broion in the Berici Hills.

Cardini's provisional sounding into the Palaeolithic levels in the great Ligurian cave of Arene Candide luckily uncovered an exceptionally rich burial which is datable to this Early Epi-Gravettian. Here was the body of a young man laid out on his back on a bed of red ochre. His face bore the traces of a fatal wound, which was covered, perhaps intentionally to hide the disfigurement, by three pointed and perforated antler objects. These objects are known in the archaeological literature by the French nineteenth-century term of *batons de commandements* since they were considered to be symbols of authority, but in fact their actual use is uncertain. A fourth *baton* lay against the man's right shoulder. Three of them were decorated with simple multilinear incisions. In his right hand the corpse held a flint knife and he had originally worn a cap of which only the many hundreds of *nassa* shells, sewn on it for decoration, survived. Shells also decorated his knee and wrist and a curious beetle-like bone amulet was found by his side. Between his body and the bed of red ochre a fine black stain was noticed which has been interpreted by the excavator as the traces of skin clothing.

The shell-ornamented cap is very similar to those on the earlier Gravettian burials from the Grimaldi caves and a whole series of similar burials in south-eastern France. The *batons de commandements* also provide a link with France being characteristic of the Magdalenian culture.

The remains of hunted game in these Early Epi-Gravettian deposits show us that this culture was flourishing in the final cold phase of the Würm glaciation (Würm III) for ibex and marmot are conspicuous at Arene Candide, and ibex and elk in the Veneto.

The Evolved Epi-Gravettian, which is the last Pleistocene culture represented in the North, flourished at the same time as the Late

Fig. 6

Plate 1

Fig. 7 Riparo Tagliente (Verona). Pebble with incised ox-head (after Mezzena). 1 : 3

Magdalenian in France and the Romanellian in southern Italy. It is characterized by some minor changes in flint technology, including the first use of the micro-burin technique which involves the production of small implements by notching and snapping blades.

The richest Upper Palaeolithic deposit so far found in the Veneto, in the rock shelter known as the Riparo Tagliente at Grezzana in the Lessini Mountains, was built up during this period and a carbon 14 date of 10,090 B C has been obtained for it.

Plate 4

A clear indication of the arrival of warmer conditions, perhaps corresponding to the Allerød oscillation in Northern Europe, is provided by the faunal remains from Riparo Tagliente which comprise mainly red deer together with a certain amount of roe deer and wild cattle. The same site has produced an enormous quantity of flint tools and waste flakes, as well as some bone points, imported sea shells and one or two pebbles scratched with outline engravings of the heads and fore-quarters of animals.

Fig. 7

Two roughly contemporary open sites have been found high in the mountains to the north of Vicenza, which seem to have been encamp-ments of hunters who were ranging just above the level of the receding glaciers. At the Riparo Battaglia, which is situated at a height of over 3000 feet near Asiago, three concentrations of flint tools and debris aligned along the foot of a limestone cliff suggest that huts or tents may have stood in this sheltered position. At the other site, Fiorentini, flint tools were found actually lying on the surface of glacial deposits, incorporated in wind-blown soils laid down under arctic conditions; a context which suggests that the ice sheets in the vicinity had started to contract with the onset of the warmer post-glacial climate by the time the hunters camped here.

Fig. 8

Fig. 8 Riparo Battaglia (Asiago). Concentrations of flint implements along the foot of a rock face possibly indicating huts. The dotted line defines the area of excavation (after Broglio)

5 m.

29

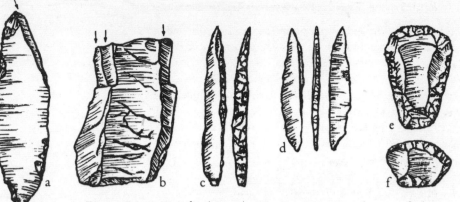

*Fig. 9 Riparo Battaglia (Asiago). Late Epi-Gravettian industry. a, b burins;
c, d backed points; e-f short blade scrapers (after Broglio). a-d actual size; e, f 2 : 3*

POST-GLACIAL HUNTING COMMUNITIES

By about 8000 B C the final cold stage of the Würm Glaciation had come
to a rapid end and it was replaced by a warmer post-glacial climate. It
was now that the scars of the retreating ice, in the shape of the broad flat
glacial valleys, the great water-filled glacier beds of Garda, Maggiore,
Como and numerous other lakes and the hilly expanses of end moraines
along the northern edge of the Plain, took on their present appearance.
These were new landscapes which were to play an important part in
influencing the distribution of subsequent prehistoric settlements.

The hunters who continued to occupy Northern Italy after the retreat
and final disappearance of the ice appear to have differed little from their
immediate Pleistocene ancestors. They continued to produce a similar
Gravettian type tool kit of small backed blades and points used as inserts
for projectiles although, as in contemporary post-glacial tool traditions
over the whole of Europe, these now show an increasing diminution in
size.

There is in fact so little basic change in cultural tradition that Italian
prehistorians prefer to use the general term Epi-Palaeolithic, rather than
the useful but perhaps misleading word Mesolithic, which is used to
describe post-glacial cultures north of the Alps. The first and principal
post-glacial culture is similarly now generally referred to as the Final
Epi-Gravettian.

Fig. 9

In Liguria many of the caves occupied during the Late Pleistocene continued to be used and the Epi-Palaeolithic remains from Arene Candide are especially interesting. The relevant layers in this cave contained ibex bones, the principal game hunted by these people, as well as abundant bird bones and carbonized seeds and fruits. Among the latter, hazel nuts, which it is worth remembering are one of the few natural vegetable foods that store over winter, were well represented.

Several extended burials were found in the same levels and these were accompanied by personal ornaments such as necklaces of perforated animal teeth and sea shells (*pectunculus*), while children sometimes had rows of squirrels tails hanging from their necks, used perhaps as a necklace or else sewn onto a cape. Most burials were also provided with small water-worn pebbles which had been coloured with red ochre. Although not decorated with patterns, these pebbles are probably related to the equally enigmatic and better known ornamented pebbles of the Azilian culture, which evolved not far away in northern Spain and south-western France. A carbon 14 date of 8380 ± 95 for these levels at Arene Candide shows too that this assemblage was roughly contemporary with the Azilian.

Plate 6

Another Epi-Palaeolithic deposit with a similar flint industry from the Ligurian coast was found in the cave of Arma dello Stefanin. Carbon 14 dates from this site are somewhat later than those from Arene Candide, being between 6850 ± 300 and 5850 ± 100 B C.

Until recently no Epi-Palaeolithic sites at all were recorded in the area of the Po Plain but in 1968 a cave deposit was found at Vatte di Zambana just north of Trento in the Adige Valley and an open site was discovered to the south of Trento at Romagnano in 1969. A series of carbon 14 dates placed the occupation of Zambana to between 6000 and 5500 B C. Broglio still calls the Zambana industry Final Epi-Gravettian, even though some new features are recognizable, the most conspicuous being the small triangular microliths which are found together with very small Gravettian-type backed points. The same deposits also contained an extended burial in red ochre.

The Romagnano site appears to be even later in date than Zambana and may be now properly called Mesolithic, for the flint industry includes trapezoid microliths for tipping arrows which in the central and western Mediterranean and other parts of Europe are distinctive of the last hunting communities (Tardenoisian) before the introduction of Neolithic farming.

Moving eastwards, we find more extensive traces of these last purely hunting communities in the limestone caves of the Trieste karst country. In the Grotta Azzurra di Samartorza laying directly below Neolithic levels are several horizons of Epi-Palaeolithic and Mesolithic deposits. In this succession it is possible to recognize a development from the lower levels, which contain the distinctive Final Epi-Gravettian tool-kit of backed bladelets and circular scrapers, to the four upper levels in which trapezoidal microliths of Tardenoisian type predominate. *Columbella* shells, used for ornaments, are found in the upper layers and it is quite probable that the *columbella* shells from Tardenoisian settlements north of the Alps in Switzerland and southern Germany were traded northwards by these people on the shores of the Adriatic.

A study of the fauna from the Grotta Azzurra shows a change in diet that is closely correlated with the changes in flint tools. In the lower levels the economy of the group inhabiting the cave was based largely on the hunting of land game, mainly deer, supplemented by sea fishing; then, in the deposits just below those in which trapezes appear for the first time, fishing starts to give way to the collection of shell-fish, mainly limpets (*patella*) and top shells (*trochus*). Finally, in the last stages of the settlement, shell-fish appear to dominate the diet entirely.

The increase in the importance of shell-fish collecting in the diets of coastal populations in Europe during the period immediately preceding the first emergence of Neolithic farming communities is a phenomenon which has so far not been adequately explained. In the Mediterranean region, from Corfu to Portugal, a whole series of coastal sites with shell middens have been identified, for the most part associated with Tardenoisian-type flint work, while similar middens are found too on the Atlantic coast of France and Britain, and across to the Ertebølle culture of Denmark.

As we shall see in the following chapter, shell-fish collection is continued in many of the initial Neolithic settlements in Italy and this provides us with evidence that indigenous populations to some extent played a part in the growth of local Neolithic cultures.

Fig. 10 Grotta Azzurra di Samartorza (Trieste). Mesolithic industry, Backed points, geometric forms, and micro-burin (after Cannarella and Cremonesi). Actual size

CHAPTER III

The First Farmers
(5000–2500 BC)

During the fifth millennium BC Italy for the first time felt the impact of the economic revolution in agriculture and animal domestication that had been spreading through Anatolia and Greece during the preceding two millennia. At the same time, the crafts of potting and polishing hard stone for axes were also introduced and later there followed improved weaving equipment and religious paraphernalia in the forms of clay stamps and figurines, likewise apparently all of eastern origin.

How far these new ideas were introduced into Italy by migrants from the countries to the east and how far they were acquired and developed by local Mesolithic peoples through trade contacts across the Adriatic, it is difficult to assess conclusively from the fragmentary archaeological record. Ruth Whitehouse has recently suggested that a combination of both factors would best explain the initial developments of the Neolithic cultures in the south of the Italian peninsula; but the evidence that is at present available from Northern Italy would indicate that it was mainly the local population who were involved in this transformation.

THE IMPRESSED WARE CULTURE

The earliest farming communities and the first pottery-making peoples in Italy belonged to the cultural tradition characterized by pottery with prolific impressed decoration which has earned it the name of the Impressed Ware Culture. Variants of this culture are to be found distributed all round the coasts of the central and western Mediterranean in caves and open sites usually located close to the sea shore. These people were clearly competent seafarers, since not only does their coastal distribution suggest that communication was mainly by water, but many of the small offshore islands like the Tremiti and the islands on the Dalmatian coast were densely settled as well.

Several authorities, among them notably Bernabò Brea, have maintained that this spread of culture resulted from an actual migration of Neolithic peoples from the eastern Mediterranean, for similar impressed

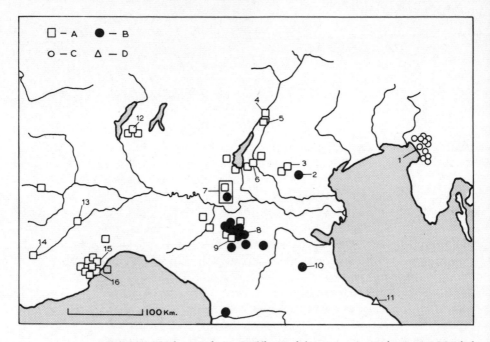

Fig. 11 Northern Italy in Middle Neolithic times. A Early Square-Mouthed pottery culture (Quinzano-Finale); B Fiorano sites; C Vlašca (Danilo); D Ripoli sites. 1 Vlašca Jama; 2 Valcalaona; 3 Molino Casarotto; 4 La Vela di Trento; 5 Romagnano; 6 Quinzano; 7 Vho; 8 Fiorano; 9 Chiozza; 10 Imola; 11 Ripa-bianca; 12 Isolino; 13 Alba; 14 Grotta Aisone; 15 Grotta Pollera; 16 Arene Candide

pottery is found at Mersin in Turkey and on sites in Syria. However, although the new techniques of pottery-making may have come from that direction, the fact that the distribution of Impressed Ware sites in the central and western Mediterranean coincides closely with that of the preceding Tardenoisian culture, and that many Impressed Ware groups even make use of the same trapezoidal flint projectile heads and have a similar diet of shell-fish, strongly suggests a local Mesolithic ancestry for these people.

Fig. 11

In Northern Italy Impressed Ware groups are represented both along the Adriatic and the Ligurian coast lines. A few sherds of characteristic pottery from the Grotta delle Gallerie constitutes the very meagre evidence for the occupation of the Trieste caves by the Impressed Ware peoples.

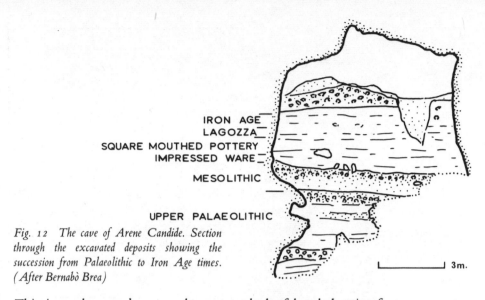

IRON AGE
LAGOZZA
SQUARE MOUTHED POTTERY
IMPRESSED WARE

MESOLITHIC

UPPER PALAEOLITHIC

Fig. 12 The cave of Arene Candide. Section through the excavated deposits showing the succession from Palaeolithic to Iron Age times. (After Bernabò Brea)

3m.

This site can however be seen as the most northerly of the whole series of Impressed Ware settlements scattered down the Dalmatian coast of which the nearest are the caves of Jamina Sredi, Vela Spilja and Vorganska Peć on the islands of Cres, Mali Losinj and Krk respectively. On the Italian shore of the Adriatic the corresponding chain of Impressed Ware settlements extends no farther north than the site of Ripabianca near Ancona.

Whereas the Impressed Ware settlements on the opposite shores of the Adriatic together constitute a single regional variant of the total Impressed Ware culture, distinguished principally by its simple bucket-shaped pots with over-all impressed ornamentation of the Molfetta style, the Ligurian Impressed Ware settlements are more closely aligned with a series of sites which extends from Liguria westwards along the southern coast of France, (cave of Châteauneuf les Martigues), and further into eastern Spain (the caves of Montserrat and the Cueva dela Sarsa).

Some eleven caves on the Ligurian coast have produced Impressed Ware finds.

The cave of Arene Candide was reoccupied during this period, following a period of abandonment since the Epi-Palaeolithic occupation, and Bernabò Brea's excavation of this approximately three-foot-thick deposit in the cave (layers 28–25), has given us the clearest picture of the Impressed Ware culture in Liguria.

Fig. 12

Fig. 13

There are two types of pot which seem to have been most in use on the site, one a deep hemispherical bowl with impressed or incised decoration and the other a large cylindrical jar ornamented with horizontal and vertical cordons. Other pot forms such as cylindrical necked jars are not so common.

The hemispherical bowls are more tastefully decorated than the indiscriminately ornamented pots of the South Italian Molfetta style, with motifs organized into simple bands and panels. The surface decoration was impressed, using the ends of small bones, animal teeth, the finger nails, or the edge of a cardium (cockle) shell, this last method being the most popular. Lines of jabbed furrows, a technique for which German archaeologists have a handy word, *Furchenstich*, and simple incisions were used as well.

Green-stone axes with pointed butts made out of a diabase rock commonly occur, but flint tools are rare owing to the absence of any suitable local flint. The trapezoidal flint arrow-head whose significance was discussed on p. 31 is, however, represented here and obsidian, probably from Sardinia, was already being brought by sea to the cave. Bone points are very numerous and pendants and necklaces were made from the teeth of pig and dog.

Although bones of domesticated cattle, sheep and pig have been identified from the cave, these peoples' economy was mainly based on hunting and collecting. The bones of red deer are common and brown bear is also well represented. Large quantities of discarded shells of limpets (*patella*) and topshell (*trochus*) remind one immediately of the late Mesolithic inhabitants of the Grotta Azzura.

The Impressed Ware levels have produced a carbon 14 date of 4270± 55 BC; this is slightly lower than the general average for Impressed Ware sites in the Mediterranean which falls around the middle of the fifth millennium.

While the Impressed Ware culture flourished on the coast, two other Neolithic cultures were emerging in the hinterland on the North Italian Plain; these are usually referred to as Fiorano and the Square-Mouthed Pottery cultures (*cultura a vasi a bocca quadrata*). Their origins are at present not entirely clear although it can be argued that in the make-up of both there is a substantial local Mesolithic element. To start with, both seem to have developed contemporaneously, the Fiorano evolving in the

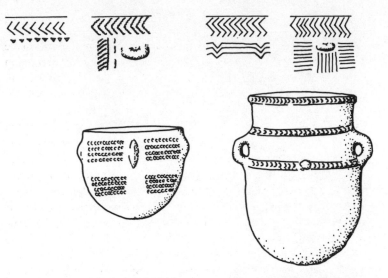

Fig. 13 Impressed Ware of the Ligurian coast. Above, characteristic decoration on bowls, done with incision cardium and 'furchenstich' techniques. Below, the two dominant pot types (after Bernabò Brea)

eastern Po Plain and the Square-Mouthed Pottery group in the west and Liguria. Later, however, at the end of the fourth millennium, the Square-Mouthed Pottery becomes dominant and Fiorano fades away.

THE FIORANO CULTURE

Although a number of sites of this culture had been excavated and published by G. Chierici before the end of the nineteenth century, it was not until 1953 that the culture as a whole was first properly defined and given a name by Fernando Malavoti of Modena.

The Fiorano settlements are for the most part concentrated along the margin of the Po Plain between Modena and Imola in Emilia, but there is a group of sites at Vhò, out in the Plain west of Mantua, and a rich but isolated site at Le Basse di Valcalaona near the Euganean Hills in the Veneto. The Sasso culture, found south and west of the Apennines in Central Italy, although closely related, is outside the scope of this book.

Fiorano settlements are all sited on low-lying terrain, and often cover extensive areas of ground. The only structural remains known from these

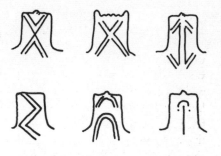

Fig. 14 Fiorano pottery. Left, bowl and handled
cup with impressed and incised decoration (after
Malavolti); right, varieties of decorated handle

sites are pits, such as have been found at Imola, Vhò, Le Basse and
Chiozza. Usually these are very regular and shallow with an oval,
circular or figure-of-eight plan. They vary in size from about 9 feet in
diameter in the case of some of the circular pits to an over-all axial length
of 27 feet for a figure-of-eight pit at Vhò. Their floors are mostly level and
usually lie at no more than about 2 feet below the original ground surface.
Exactly what these pits were used for is unclear and, in the absence of
other structural remains from Fiorano sites, many Italian prehistorians
still maintain that they represent the excavated floors of huts (*fondi di
capanne*). The lack of post-holes perhaps makes this interpretation seem
unlikely, and it is more probable that they were used for storage of grain
or other materials, as was the practice elsewhere in prehistoric Europe.

Fondi di capanne are not restricted to Fiorano but are a feature of several
other Neolithic cultures in Italy where they are again the only kind of
internal settlement feature present, and we shall be returning to the
problem of the interpretation of these pits later. Two pits of a different
kind were also found at Vhò. These were 13 and 14 feet deep respectively, and little more than 3 feet wide, and are probably best explained
as wells.

Both domesticated and wild animals were present in the settlements
although in what proportions is not quite clear. The nature of Fiorano
burial customs is also uncertain: one or two isolated crouched inhumation burials have been attributed to this tradition (Calerno and
S. Ilario d'Enza, both in Emilia) but they are without grave goods.

The pottery and stone tools found in these Fiorano sites are remarkably uniform and distinctive. The standard range of pots used in the villages was made in a fine brown or grey ware and comprised carinated cups with bossed strap handles, open rounded bowls with loop handles, and large bucket-shaped cooking or storage vessels. In addition there were a few globular vessels with cylindrical necks, which are perhaps copies of fine buff-ware flasks imported from the Ripoli culture of Central Italy, sherds of which have also been found on some sites. The cups and some of the bowls and flasks are attractively decorated with rather bizarre geometric motifs, composed of broad incised lines and small, oval, grain-like impressions. Some of these designs may be interpreted as stylized human figures. The larger bucket-shaped vessels are by contrast usually adorned with verticle rib-like cordons.

Fig. 14

Plate 10

The flint tools were manufactured exclusively from parallel-sided blades and comprise a limited range of types among which the rhomboid arrow-heads, awls, end-scrapers and angle burins are the most characteristic. A very unusual type of burin (the Ripabianca burin) also occurs, and is unique in the whole of European prehistory, having the chisel cutting edge in a notch at the side of the blade. Pressure-flaked artifacts are completely absent.

Fig. 15

Fig. 15 Fiorano Culture flint work. End scraper, rhomboid and 'Ripabianca' burin from Le Basse di Valcalaona (after Barfield and Broglio). Actual size

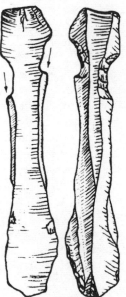

Plates 8, 9

Polished stone axes, jade bracelets with a triangular cross-section, and clay figurines are known from some sites.

Carbon 14 dates of 4050±200 BC for the Fiorano culture have now been obtained from Chiozza and of 4310±85 and 4260±75 BC from Ripabianca, near Ancona, where Fiorano-type flint tools were found with Impressed Ware Culture pottery.

The material remains of this culture betray little as to the ultimate origin of their makers. Techniques of pottery decoration and motifs hint at possible contact with the Danubian Linear Pottery tradition; bossed strap handles and figurines, however, point to the eastern Mediterranean, while rhomboid flints and burins might suggest a European Mesolithic background.

SQUARE-MOUTHED POTTERY

To the west and north of the Fiorano culture, in the Po Plain and in Liguria, another equally distinctive tradition emerged, making its debut towards the end of the fifth millennium. Far less uniform in character and having a much longer and more complex life than Fiorano, the Square-Mouthed Pottery culture confronts us with a large number of problems both in its chronology and its regional classification.

However, three main stages of this culture's development have recently been identified in the Veneto and it is likely that three corresponding phases can also be recognized in Emilia.

This threefold scheme can in fact probably be applied with caution to the whole of Northern Italy. The first period is represented in Liguria and in the Po Plain as far east as Fimon near Vicenza (Veneto) and at Mezzavia di Sassuolo in Emilia. A convenient name for this phase of development is Finale-Quinzano after Arene Candide at Finale in Liguria, and Quinzano, one of the principal sites in the Veneto. For the most part this stage flourished contemporaneously with Fiorano although in western Emilia it probably replaced Fiorano.

Sites of this phase were varied in character. In Liguria, for example, cave sites alone are recorded, notably Arene Candide (levels 24–14) and Pollera, but in the Po Plain open settlements are the rule. The latter are either villages on level ground on the margin of the Plain, like Quinzano or, more distinctively, villages on the edge of lakes, as at Molino Casarotto (Fimon) and Frassine near Peschiera.

Fig. 16   Molino Casarotto. Part of wooden 'bonifica' platform and hearths of early Square-Mouthed Pottery settlement, 18 m. across

The recent excavations at Molino Casarotto (1969–70) by the universities of Ferrara and Birmingham have thrown a lot more light on the Finale-Quinzano phase. Four or five small settlement areas, perhaps each occupied by a single family group, were found here scattered along the former margin of a lake. One of these areas was completely cleared revealing a cluster of roughly rectangular timber floors with associated verticle piles and hearths. Together with the scatter of rubbish these structures covered an area some 45 feet in diameter. A tentative interpretation might suggest that we are here in the presence of an L-shaped hut, although it should be admitted that the posts surrounding the floors may have been inserted for strengthening the horizontal timbers rather

Plate 12

Fig. 16

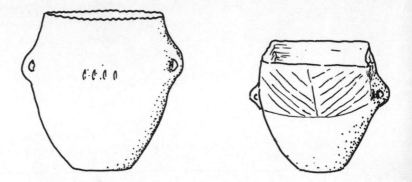

than as wall supports. Constructed on one of the platforms was a massive circular hearth of stone which had been rebuilt at least six times. These, perhaps annual renewals, could in some instances be related to the periodic rebuilding of the surrounding platform.

Middens of discarded freshwater mollusc shells, mainly mussel but also containing pike and turtle bones, dumps of pottery and animal bones were found on the landward side of the platforms.

The economy of the settlement clearly relied mainly on hunting and collecting, for besides the middens, red deer was overwhelmingly the commonest animal on the site. Domesticated sheep and cattle were represented only in small quantities. The numerous bones of pig could either be wild or domesticated species. Wild vegetable foods were also well represented, especially the husks of water chestnuts which still grow profusely in the Lake of Fimon today. Cultivated cereals were found in small quantities and grape pips, the earliest to have been found in Italy, were also recovered.

The stratigraphy of the hearth showed that layers of pure shell midden alternated with water-chestnut deposits perhaps indicating seasonal collecting activity, while the periodic reconstruction of the hearth could well be evidence of the site being temporarily abandoned, probably during the winter months.

It is also interesting to note that in Liguria the cave of Arma di Nasino produced evidence of a diet almost exclusively of wild game, and of the collection of cockle shells during the Square-Mouthed Pottery phase.

Traces of an inhumation cemetery were recognized near the Molino Casarotto village. Better preserved graves were excavated by Zorzi at Quinzano, where crouched burials were accompanied by pots, arrows

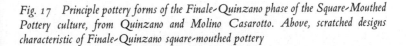

Fig. 17 *Principle pottery forms of the Finale-Quinzano phase of the Square-Mouthed Pottery culture, from Quinzano and Molino Casarotto. Above, scratched designs characteristic of Finale-Quinzano square-mouthed pottery*

and stone axes. In Liguria a total of 30 burials has been found in the cave of Arene Candide and 42 in the Pollera cave. Of these it is recorded that some 24 adults were represented as against 15 children and infants, a ratio which compares closely with mortality figures worked out from other Neolithic cemeteries in Europe. In these graves the adults were enclosed in stone cists and had grave-goods of pottery, stone and bone tools and ornaments of animal teeth and shell, while the infant graves were usually without any protection or finds.

The fine, usually black, burnished pottery found on sites from Liguria to the Veneto is all very similar, comprising shallow conical bowls with flat bases, pots with short or tall pedestals and square-mouthed beaker-like drinking vessels and larger square-mouthed jars. The pedestal-pots and the square-mouthed beakers are usually decorated with geometric motifs finely incised on the pottery just before firing when the clay was leather hard. These motifs comprise ladder patterns, hatched triangles, lozenges and zig-zag bands. Although this fine pottery is everywhere very uniform, there is a considerable difference between the coarse pottery found in Liguria and that of the Po Plain. In Liguria, cooking and storage pots are undecorated and the principal form is a large cylindrical-necked, pear-shaped jar with three strap handles, while in the Veneto and Emilia we find a distinctive series of matt-surfaced, bucket-shaped, square-mouthed pots decorated with an upper register of simple incised patterns and barrel-shaped jars with serrated rims and 'dragged stick' impressions on their surfaces.

This potting tradition seems to owe little to outside cultural influence although the scratched designs might possibly be related to the Neolithic Matera style of Southern Italy and the impressed barrel jars of the Po

Plates 13, 14

43

Valley may ultimately have been derived from the Impressed Ware culture. It is in any case highly improbable that the square-mouthed pot forms were in any way influenced by the cultures of the Danube basin as has been maintained over many years. For one thing eastern parallels are neither numerous nor convincing and moreover in the lower levels at Arene Candide it is possible to see in fact a development from pots with mouths pinched in on four sides in a quadrilobate shape to those with a true square opening, suggesting local evolution of the square-mouthed pot from a round-mouthed form.

Flasks of fine buff (*figulina*) ware were imported from Southern and Central Italy as they were to Fiorano sites. Some of these were even painted with characteristic southern designs, such as the fragment with Ripoli-style hatched panels and dotted border from Caverna dell'Acqua in Liguria, flask necks with Ripoli multilinear motifs from Chiozza, and Capri-style motifs on sherds from Arene Candide. The prevalence of flask forms in this alien buff ware possibly suggests that they were imported from the south filled, one would like to think, with wine or oil.

Plate 11

Arrow-heads of a long triangular tanged type with pressure-flaked retouch are common and other flint tools include burins, end-scrapers and awls, all usually manufactured from well made blades. Two arrows found at Molino Casarotto still had part of their wooden shaft and bound clay matrix for the flint point preserved intact. It is interesting to note the scarcity of waste flakes at Molino Casarotto and Arene Candide, indicating that tools were imported to these sites ready made.

Fig. 18

Besides polished stone axes, small stone chisels with a D-shaped cross-section were used and triangular-sectioned bracelets made of a variety of stone are common in Liguria.

Plate 19

Other equipment includes clay stamps or *pintaderas*, which were probably used for decorating the body, and clay figurines, usually interpreted, rightly or wrongly, as representing a fertility goddess. It is worth noticing that there appears to be more than a chance association between clay figurines and clay stamps on Neolithic sites, over most of the area in which they have been found, an area which includes Anatolia, the Balkans and Greece as well as Italy. This suggests that both objects were used together for a definite cult purpose and points to a widespread community of religious belief. A series of perforated human teeth found at Molino Casarotto may also have had some ritual significance.

Bone tools are common, especially on the Ligurian coast, where flint is rare, and we find in the same area shell fish-hooks and even trumpets made from triton shell. Pendants of animal teeth, shells and other natural objects are also recorded; one of the Pollera burials was even provided with a necklace made from the greater part of the skeleton of a lynx.

A series of six dates from Molino Casarotto, falling between 4520 and 4175 BC, are the earliest we have for the Square-Mouthed Pottery culture and puts its origins contemporary with both the Impressed Ware and Fiorano traditions. Other dates for this first stage are somewhat later; Arene Candide 3515±50 (layers 16–19) 3385±50 (layers 21–24); Grotta Aisone (Piedmont) 3875±75 BC.

The origins of the Square-Mouthed Pottery culture are as difficult to fathom as are those of the Fiorano group. The shell middens and hunting economy of Molino Casarotto might indicate a descent from local Mesolithic stock. On the other hand, however, various East Mediterranean ideas such as figurines and *pintaderas* and of course the whole gamut of Neolithic farming and technology may well have been adopted by a native population. A probable connection existed too between this culture and its eastern neighbour the Danilo culture of the Dalmatian coast which shares similar stone chisels and tanged arrow-heads. The similarities in the ceramic tradition with southern Italy have already been mentioned.

The second stage of the Square-Mouthed Pottery culture has been clearly identified in the Veneto, where it is represented in the initial occupation of the Rocca di Rivoli (Rivoli-Spiazzo phase) and in Emilia where the principal occupation of the long-lived settlement of Chiozza, as well as the first occupation of the site of Pescale, belong to this phase. The choice of naturally fortified hill-tops, strategically dominating river

Plate 15

Plate 21

Fig. 18 Polished stone axe from Alba Cuneo (Piedmont) with incised geometric motifs on the blade (after Lo Porto). 3 : 4

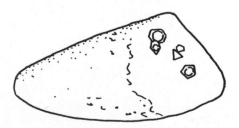

routes as at Rivoli and Pescale marks a divergence from the types of settlement location listed for the Finale-Quinzano phase, and it may reflect the
increasing importance of trade routes or an unstable political climate.

Some of the burnt-clay floors and pits found at Chiozza certainly
belong to this stage of development and a cemetery of nineteen crouched
burials from the same site may be contemporary, although precise
attribution is uncertain owing to the lack of closely datable grave goods.
Only eight of the graves had, in fact, been provided with objects and
these consisted of polished stone axes, flint arrow-heads, and necklaces
and bracelets made from dentalium shell and steatite beads.

Another cemetery consisting of three cist burials and probably also
dating to this period was found at Vela near Trento on the River Adige.
The graves again had no pottery, but were provided with a fine series of
tanged triangular arrow-heads and a jade axe. A shoe-last adze found in
the same cemetery points to contact with the Neolithic cultures lying to
the north of the Alps, and is the earliest certain evidence that we have for
the use of the Central Alpine passes.

The main difference between this and the preceding phase is to be seen
in the fine-ware pottery. Square-mouthed beakers and square-mouthed
jars are now no longer produced, but wide square-mouthed bowls,
of a type which are rare in the earlier phase, now become common and

Fig. 19

are richly decorated with swag designs round the corners and side panels.
The decoration was scratched, incised or set in relief by cutting away the
surface background (again a German term *Kerbschnitt* is a useful one for

Plate 17

describing this technique) and the new motifs comprise a variety of spiral
patterns, sausage-like patterns, hatched bands, dot-filled triangles and
barbed-wire lines. Also new are deep rounded bowls, with beaded rims
and decorated with bands of running spirals. The range of coarse ware
on the other hand remains essentially the same as it was in the Finale
Quinzano phase.

There are striking similarities between the bead-rim bowls and the
running-spiral designs from Rivoli-Spiazzo and Chiozza and the
pottery of the Dalmatian Danilo culture.

In Lombardy the middle levels of the lake village of Isolino probably
date to this period, although the square-mouthed bowls here have a
different range of incised designs. Obsidian blades, which analysis has
shown were imported from Sardinia, have been found on this site.

Fig. 19   Chiozza style pottery and cut out decoration. a Bowl with beaded rim from Chiozza; b Square-mouthed bowl from Pescale; c Cut out motifs; d Lid from Chiozza

The square-mouthed pottery assemblage at Isolino was stratified above a lower settlement horizon associated with a platform of corduroy-laid timbers, similar to the one found at Molino Casarotto. This lower deposit contained decorated pedestal vessels, cups and other pottery which do not include any with square mouths, and it may well be seen as a completely separate cultural complex. Radiocarbon dates from the platform and just above it are 3584±144 BC and 3376±180 BC respectively.

The third and final stage of the Square-Mouthed Pottery culture has so far been found only in Emilia and the Veneto and it is probable that further west the people responsible for the Lagozza culture had already ousted the square-mouthed pottery tradition. In Emilia there is one site, Pescale, which has produced a type of pottery so far not known elsewhere in Italy, pottery which can be called typical of a Pescale sub-culture. Deep bowls, with a quadrilobate rather than a square mouth, were in vogue here and these, together with open bowls and bucket-shaped pots, are decorated with a limited range of incised cross-hatched bands, hatched arcading and herring-bone patterns running between horizontal lines. Sardinian obsidian was imported in some quantity to Pescale probably during this period.

Fig. 21

Plate 16

In the Veneto there is a series of sites of this final phase with material and pottery, rather different from Pescale, which can be called the Rivoli-Castelnovo group. Characteristic sites are mainly now in strategic hill positions (Rivoli, Castelnovo, Isera), but caves (Bocca Lorenza), open sites (Vhò) and marsh settlements (Palu della Santissima) are also found.

Large and small circular pits with flat bottoms are the main structural features on the Rocca di Rivoli, and like the Fiorano examples discussed earlier these are most likely to have been used for storage. The only traces of huts were the damaged clay hearths and a dump of burnt daub which included a number of pieces decorated by channelling. These fragments had originally been applied to the surface of square and round cross-sectioned timbers and would have given the effect of fluted columns.

Plate 18

Early fired-clay weaving equipment to be used in northern Italy comes from this horizon at Rivoli and includes decorated spindle whorls and heavy conical and cylindrical loom weights. One of the finest figurines of the Italian Neolithic was also found in a Rivoli-Castelnovo pit at Rivoli and *pintaderas* too continued in use.

Fig. 20

The pottery from all Rivoli-Castelnovo sites is very standardized, deep square-mouthed (or rather, now, quadrilobate in outline) bowls being the most characteristic form. Two varieties of this bowl type are found, one matt-surfaced with panels of herring-bone incisions, the other having a burnished surface with rows of incised hatched triangles. Coarse pottery is dominated by the barrel- or bucket-shaped vessels with undulating rims and triple plastic knobs. Conical clay funnels with sieve perforations, perhaps for making cheese or boiling milk, standard kitchen equipment which last well into the Bronze Age in the North, also make their appearance during this stage.

Fig. 20 Pottery of the Late Square-Mouthed Pottery Culture. a Bowl from Pescale; b Rivoli-Castelnovo bowl from Rivoli; c Milk boiler from Pescale; (a and c after Malavolti)

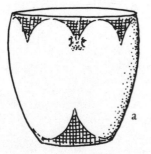

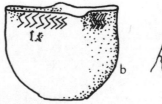

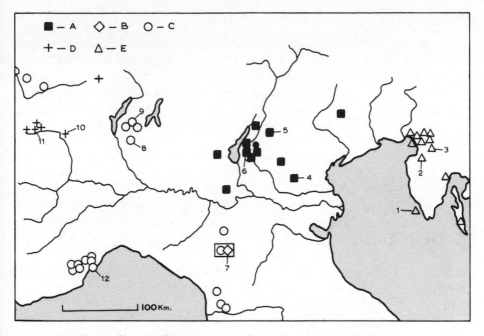

Fig. 21   Distribution of Late Neolithic sites. A Rivoli-Castelnovo sites; B Pescale;
C Lagozza and Chassey sites; D Cist graves; E Brijuni-Škocjan; 1 Brijuni;
2 Grotta delle Gallerie; 3 Škocjanska Jama; 4 Castelnovo di Teolo; 5 Bocca
Lorenza; 6 Rivoli; 7 Pescale; 8 Lagozza; 9 Isolino; 10 Montjovet; 11 Villeneuve;
12 Arene Candide

Masses of flint was quarried locally and worked on the spot at Rivoli
but the tools were of an inferior quality to those produced in previous
stages of the culture and were mainly on flakes, in contrast to the earlier
blade industries. The same range of artifacts is represented but it is
interesting to note that the previously popular tanged arrow-head is
replaced at Rivoli by leaf-shaped points. Small polished stone axes are
found, including examples made of jade.

The bone tools from Rivoli have a distinctly Mesolithic character
including as they do knives made of boars' tusks, an antler adze and an
example of the 'groove and splinter' technique of cutting up antler.

A small fragment of copper was found in these levels at Rivoli while,
in the cave of Bocca Lorenza in the eastern Lessini Mountains, three
trapezoid copper axes were found apparently associated with square-

Plate 20

mouthed pottery of Rivoli-Castelnovo type. These are probably the earliest metal objects to be made in the north, probably from local ores, and herald the dawn of the new era of metal.

The animal bones from Rivoli consist of cattle, pig and red deer in roughly equal proportions, which shows that hunting was still important. Carbonized acorns also demonstrate a continued reliance on collected wild fruits.

The trans-alpine contacts and the first use of the Central Alpine passes, already hinted at in the shoe-last adze from Vela, is confirmed during this late phase at Rivoli by an imported fragment of 'stab-and-drag' ornamented pottery typical of the south German Aichbühl culture while a group of the coarse pottery with arcaded rim decoration similar to products of the Michelsberg culture along the Northern Alps is also found.

Exactly when the Rivoli-Castelnovo period, the last stage of the Square-Mouthed Pottery culture, came to an end is at present difficult to say. It was apparently flourishing during the last half of the fourth millennium and possibly lasted into the third.

LAGOZZA

On the Ligurian coast and to the west of the Northern Plain, the Square-mouthed Pottery culture was replaced, by 3000 BC, by a completely different tradition known as the Lagozza culture.

Although many of the same settlement sites continued in occupation, including the cave of Arene Candide (levels 13–9) and the lake village of Isolino, the artifacts of pottery and stone show almost no connection with the Square-Mouthed Pottery culture.

The affinities of this group are in fact clearly with the Chassey culture of France and western Switzerland and the evidence that is so far available would suggest that these new ideas were introduced by migrants who entered Lombardy by way of the Upper Rhône valley and the Great St Bernard pass and simultaneously pushed in along the Ligurian coast from Provence.

The principal site of the Lagozza culture is the settlement which has given its name to the culture, Lagozza di Besnate, discovered in 1875 in a peat-filled moraine basin between Milan and the Lombard lakes. Pompeo Castelfranco here uncovered the remains of a village consisting

Fig. 22   Characteristic Lagozza pottery from the type site

of a roughly rectangular area of wooden piles, measuring about 300 by
105 feet.

Lagozza pottery has a distinctive range of forms in a well-made black   *Fig. 22*
burnished fine ware. Low carinated or s-profiled bowls and deeper
bag-shaped pots are the most usual vessels. These are always undecorated
but in Lombardy the bag-shaped pots are provided with pairs of
perforated lugs and on sites in Liguria with rows of close-set cylindrical
lugs, graphically termed 'pan-pipe'. The only decoration occurs on small
plates and consists of dotted, scratched and incised motifs restricted to the
flat, internally accentuated rim. The main coarse-ware pot is a bucket-
shaped vessel. There is a regional difference between the examples of these
found in Liguria and those from Lombardy since the former are undecorated with rounded bases and the latter have flat bases and liberally
applied ornamental bosses. Conical, perforated clay 'milk boilers', like
those found at Rivoli, were also used.

Another link with Rivoli is to be found in the weaving equipment,   *Fig. 23*
with almost identical radially decorated spindle whorls, and similar
conical loom weights. The commonest type of loom weight at Lagozza
however was of a rather unusual kidney shape, with suspension on holes
at either end.

The flint industry at Lagozza, represented by blades with bilateral
retouch and transverse arrow-heads, is very different from that of the

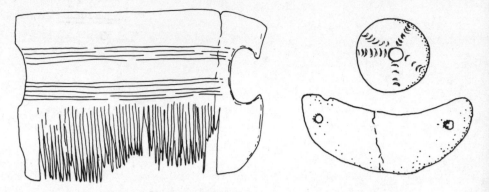

Fig. 23   Decorated spindle whorl, kidney-shaped loom weight and wooden comb. All from Lagozza (after Guerreschi)

Fig. 23

Square-Mouthed Pottery tradition, but comparable to that of Chassey across the Alps.

A fine single-sided wooden comb virtually identical to the one from the Neolithic lake village of Egolzwyl in Switzerland, and some curved *batons,* which may well be throwing-sticks, are among the wooden artifacts preserved at Lagozza.

It is quite probable that metal was also used by the Lagozza people, since copper objects have been found on contemporary Swiss Chassey sites and at Attiggio, a Lagozza outpost near Ancona in the Marche. A hoard of flat copper axes found at Isolino, although unstratified, possibly relates to the Lagozza phase of occupation at that site.

In spite of the fact that the majority of features in the make-up of Lagozza can be best traced to the Chassey culture in France, the clay weaving apparatus is a North Italian and East Alpine phenomenon, appearing as it does in the late Square-Mouthed Pottery culture. Weaving gear of clay and 'milk boilers' are found for the first time too in the contemporary South Italian Diana culture and there is evidence that both may ultimately have come from the eastern Mediterranean.

Animal bones were strangely absent at Lagozza although vegetable food was well preserved and included grains of cultivated wheat (*triticum vulgare, t. dicoccum, t. monococcum, t. compactum*), barley (*hordeum vulgare, h. hexastichum*), lentils and flax, as well as wild nuts and berries like the Cornel cherry, beech mast and acorns.

Although no burials have been found on any of the main Lagozza sites, there is a group of crouched inhumation cemeteries in the upper Aosta valley just below the Great St Bernard Pass. The largest of these is at Villeneuve with at least 25 inhumation burials in stone cists; others have been excavated at Montjovet, Sarre and St Nicolas. In spite of the scarcity of grave goods – a few perforated sea shells, scraps of flint and a fragment of jade axe – the fact that similar cist cemeteries of the Chassey culture are found just across the St Bernard Pass in the Upper Rhône valley allows us to equate these with both Chassey and Lagozza.

Five of the six carbon 14 dates from Lagozza fall between 3030± 50 and 2630± 50 B C. The start of Lagozza may be contemporary with the final stages of the Square-Mouthed Pottery tradition in the Veneto, since imported Lagozza pottery appears at Rivoli. However, in the west it seems to have survived alongside and peripheral to the developing Copper Age cultures described in the next chapter, and it later played some part in the formation of the Early Bronze Age Polada culture.

THE TRIESTE CAVES

Following the Impressed Ware occupation of the caves on the Trieste Karst, we find evidence of a Neolithic development in the area which has little connection with that on the Po Plain.

At the time when the Square-Mouthed Pottery and Fiorano traditions were flourishing to the west, many of the Trieste caves (Vlašca, Teresina, Ciclami) were occupied by people belonging to a northern and rather impoverished branch of the Dalmatian Danilo culture. The differences between this particular band of cave dwellers and the main Danilo culture to the south justifies our identifying them as a distinct regional group of Danilo, which can be named after the cave of Vlašca. Their pottery is not nearly as richly decorated as at classic Danilo sites and in fact there are only one or two fragments with the more exuberant incised or painted Danilo designs. The commonest form of Vlašca pot is the deep oval bowl with a small pedestal, and a beaded rim usually decorated with a line of hatched triangle designs. Danilo-type cult vessels, 'rhyta' as they are called by the prehistorians, looking rather like coal scuttles, are represented; although these were decorated, not in the usual Danilo fashion with meander patterns, but with 'barbed wire' lines and hatched chevron bands.

Plate 22

The faunal remains from the Ciclami cave are mainly those of sheep or goat, with some cattle, pig and red deer. The cave of Vlaša, on the other hand, produced enormous quantities of limpet shells (*Patella*) which seem to relate to the Neolithic levels, and molluscs were common in the Grotta Teresina.

The Vlaša tradition was replaced during the Late Neolithic by what I have called the Brijuni–Škocjan culture, which is also confined mainly to caves. Although the two type sites Brijuni (Breoni) and Škocjan (San Canziano) are in Jugoslav territory, the Grotta delle Gallerie in Italy just south of Trieste has a large amount of typical material.

The pottery of this phase can be seen to be strongly influenced by the Baden culture, which engulfed Czechoslovakia and parts of Austria, Hungary and Jugoslavia during the third millennium BC. This is the first evidence that we have of the subsequent, almost continuous, presence of Central European influence at the head of the Adriatic around Trieste and it perhaps reflects the establishment of an outlet for Central European trade with the Mediterranean, via the Postojna pass.

This Baden influence is recognizable in a series of distinctive rounded bowls with vertically perforated, subcutaneous lugs and either plain or channelled burnished surfaces, as well as in the coarser pottery, with grass brushed, non slip surfaces. Both these ceramic styles had a wide distribution east of the Julian Alps during the third millennium.

Long distance contacts also with regions to the west and south, are evidenced by Lagozza style pottery from Brijuni and sherds of the Dalmatian Hvar culture in the Grotta Teresina, while an obsidian flake from Vlaša, probably deriving from the Late Neolithic occupation levels, has been shown by Renfrew and Cann, using the chemical trace analysis, to come from the Pontine Islands in the Tyrrhenian sea.

Stone tools are not common in either the Vlaša or Brijuni complexes, since suitable raw materials are not locally available. Copper, however, was now in use for the first time, daggers and axes being found at Brijuni and Škocjan.

Shell middens on the shore at Isola Salina on Brijuni show the survival of an economy going back to Mesolithic times and cattle, goat, pig and also deer have been recorded from the same site.

CHAPTER IV

Early Metal-using Communities of the Copper Age (2500–1800 BC)

As we have seen, a few copper tools were known to the Late Neolithic communities of the Po Plain but these were exceedingly rare. By the mid-third millennium, however, cultures were emerging in which metal tools were almost as common as stone equipment; these groups can therefore be said to belong to a Copper Age or Chalcolithic Period.

The definition of culture areas is particularly difficult during this phase of development in Northern Italy, owing to the ever-increasing variety of foreign ideas which were penetrating to the Po Plain from all four points of the compass and blurring clear-cut cultural boundaries.

REMEDELLO

The main focus of settlement during the Copper Age seems to have been the central area of the Po Plain, where a number of sites have come to light. Most of these are cemeteries and include Remedello, Fontanella and Villafranca, all to the north of the River Po, and Cumarola, Santa Ilario d'Enza, Borgo Rivola and Bosco di Malta along the edge of the Apennines, south of the Po.

Fig. 25

Similarities in stone and metal equipment from the graves allow us to group these cemeteries under one heading, the Remedello culture, after the largest of these sites, Remedello di Sotto in the province of Brescia.

At least 119 burials were excavated at the type site during the nineteenth century. The undisturbed adult graves were accompanied by the following assortment of grave goods, which are here listed in order of frequency of their occurrence: bifacially retouched, tanged arrows in 24 graves (sometimes there were as many as 11 of these in one grave and from their position it can be seen that they were originally in quivers); finely flaked, flint daggers in 16 graves; stone axes in 7 graves; copper daggers or halberds in 5 graves; trapezoidal copper axes in 4 graves and copper awls in 2 graves. In addition there was a copper bangle, a silver

Plate 25

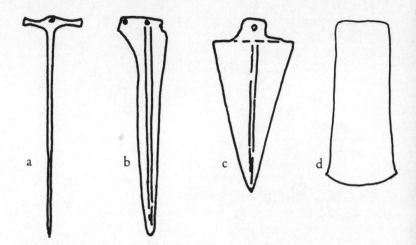

*Fig. 24 Examples of Copper Age metalwork. a Silver pin from Remedello;
b Halberd of Gambara type from Gambara; c Copper blade of Remedello type from
Panesella; d Axe from Brabbia (Lombardy)*

pin, a marble cruciform object and a collection of shell plaques which
had probably been sewn onto the fringe of a garment for ornament. Only
9 graves, those of women, contained pottery vessels of any sort. Children
were usually provided with no more than a flint knife.

The next largest cemeteries, Cumarola with at least 40 and Fontanella
with some 36 burials, produced a similar range of grave goods, as did
the smaller cemeteries mentioned earlier.

As we can see, stone axes and daggers were still more common at
Remedello than the same types made in metal. The large flint daggers
with rounded or tanged heels may well have been produced as an answer
to the new metal forms, which they appear to copy, for we can suppose
that there may have been considerable competition between the traditional flint knappers and the new metalworkers during this period of
technological transition.

Fig. 24

Plate 24

Among the copper objects, the dagger and halberd blades tell us most
about the sources of inspiration for our North Italian copper technology,
since two of the four main types that were manufactured here – the
triangular Villafranca blade with a straight rivetted heel and the
Remedello blade, which has a similar triangular outline but is provided
with a rivetted tang – both bear a close resemblance to daggers found in

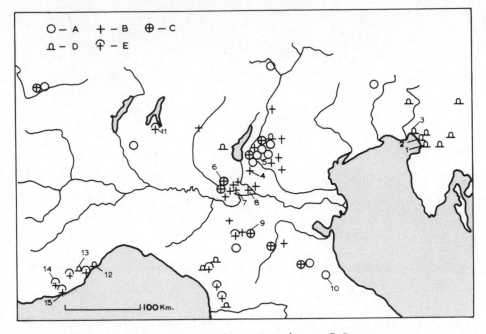

Fig. 25 Map of Copper Age sites. A Open settlement; B Single grave; C Cemetery; D Cave settlement; E Burial cave; 1 Čotarjova Jama; 2 Vlašca Jama; 3 Grotta Teresina; 4 Villafranca; 5 Le Colombare; 6 Remedello; 7 Santa Cristina and Ca' di Marco; 8 Fontanella; 9 Cumarola; 10 Panighina; 11 Buco della Sabbia; 12 Arene Candide; 13 Toirano; 14 Arma della Gra di Marmo; 15 Tana Bertrand

the Aegean and Anatolia at the end of the third millennium. There is evidence that some of these blades were hafted as halberds rather than as daggers and the Gambara type of blade was certainly designed intentionally for this purpose.

There are two silver objects which reveal something more about the external relations of the Remedello group. One is the hammer-headed pin from Remedello itself, which copies a type of pin popular among the Corded Ware peoples of Eastern and Central Europe, and the other is the beautifully-made sheet-silver chest ornament (pectoral), embossed with a fringe of dots, which came from the grave of Villafranca. A comparable pectoral is known from the Baden culture cemetery of Velvary in Czechoslovakia, although technologically it also bears a

Fig. 24, a

Plate 23

close resemblance to ornaments that were being made in the Aegean at the end of the third millennium.

Both the copper and the silver were probably mined in the Central Alpine foothills, where deposits of these metals are known from areas lying to the east and the west of the River Adige.

Plate 25

Other foreign elements in Remedello are to be recognized in the knobbed stone battle-axe of Central Italian Rinaldone type from the Cumarola cemetery, in the elbow-handled cup from Remedello, which has South Italian prototypes, and in the carinated bowls with incised metope decoration, again from Remedello, which are very similar to the pottery of the Fontbouïsse culture of southern France.

Settlements relating to the Remedello group are rare by comparison with the number of cemeteries. At Remedello part of a settlement ditch was recorded near the cemetery, but the best documented site is Le Colombare, a hill settlement north of Verona, with a fine commanding view over the Po Plain. It was excavated by F. Zorzi, who claims to have recognized eight huts built up against large outcrops of natural limestone.

Fig. 26

Only one of these was excavated, however, turning out to be a rectangular structure measuring approximately 17 by 8 feet, well built with dry stone walling.

Fig. 27

The pottery from Le Colombare included the Fontbouïsse-style bowls, like those found at Remedello, as well as large, low, rounded bowls with

Fig. 26   Plan of Copper Age House at Colombare 17 × 8 ft (after Zorzi)

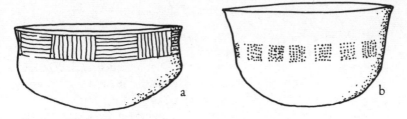

Fig. 27 Two bowls from Le Colombare: a showing influence of the Fontbouisse culture; b with dotted decoration similar to the Conelle style

impressed 'c' motifs and dotted designs, the latter reminiscent of the Conelle Copper Age culture of the Marche. There was also a range of large cooking pots with plain cordon decoration.

Flint tools were abundant, since we are here right on the edge of the flint-bearing limestone of the Lessini Mountains. Flint daggers and arrow-heads of Remedello type were associated with leaf-shaped arrow-heads of local Neolithic ancestry, as well as with a large number of roughly worked flint axes and chisels made on cores. These flint axes were long ago misleadingly named 'Campignian' on account of their similarity to axes produced at Campigny in France, even though there can have been no connection between the two areas. A better term for these objects would in fact be 'Lessinian' since their distribution is limited to the flint-bearing mountains of the Veneto, far beyond which they were never traded. Localized core-axe industries are not restricted to the Lessini Mountains, since a very similar phenomenon is found, at about this time, in the Gargano peninsula in Southern Italy.

Other finds from Le Colombare include a fragmentary stone shaft-hole battle axe, a winged limestone bead of the type that was popular in the southern French Fontbouïsse culture and, of copper, an axe, a wire ring and two awls.

Some years ago L. Zambotti suggested that the Remedello culture represented an intrusive bow-using people of Iberian origin, but today this hypothesis is really no longer acceptable. The elements forming Remedello can in fact be traced to many different foreign sources, notably the south of France and the eastern Mediterranean, while certain features such as the flat cemeteries and the tanged arrow-heads look very much like a legacy from the local Square-Mouthed Pottery culture.

59

Northern Italy

Little is known about the Chalcolithic peoples of south-eastern Emilia, although there is one remarkable site which suggests that the Conelle culture of the Marche had outposts established in this area. In 1870 when a new well shaft was being sunk at the spa of La Panighina (Forli), to tap a new sulphur spring, workmen came upon the remains of an ancient well which went down to some 30 feet below the present ground surface.

Fig. 28

This early well had a central shaft made from sections of hollow tree trunks, round which an open catchment area had been constructed by means of radiating wooden struts. The pots recovered from the bottom of the well comprised, principally, handled flagons and buckets with tubular spouts, both of which are typical Conelle culture forms. One of the flagons was in addition decorated with comb-dotted panels, again a typical Conelle motif.

The Panighina wells are still famous for their sulphurous water, which we must suppose were already a local attraction at the end of the third millennium BC.

COPPER-USING PEOPLES OF LIGURIA AND THE TRIESTE KARST

A quite separate Copper Age tradition can be recognized on the Ligurian coast and in parts of western Lombardy. This is represented by a series of small cave sites which had been used for collective inhumation burial. Both the collective burial rite and the grave goods which accompany the dead point to a continuation of the cultural link with the south of France that these areas enjoyed during the Lagozza period. Most of the caves are very small with a ground plan in which a narrow entrance passage leads into a small chamber, reminding one very much of the Megalithic passage graves that were built by the relatives of these early Ligurians not far away in south-western France.

Plate 27

The most spectacular of these Ligurian burial caves are the Tana Bertrand (Badaluco) which housed at least 10 burials, Le Camere with 12 burials and the Arma della Gra di Marmo (Realdo) with a large deposit of human bones.

The grave goods consist mainly of beads and ornaments. Tana Bertrand produced over 300 beands of calcite, haematite, copper, slate and dentalium shell. Some of the calcite beads were carved into the winged and 'single drop' types and small pendants were also made from frag-

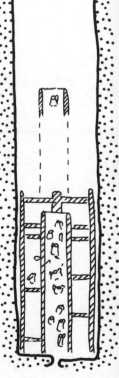

Fig. 28 Well at La Panighina, 10 m. deep, with wooden lining and Conelle pottery, and a Conelle-style flagon from the Panighina well (after Ugolini)

ments of boars' tusks. Lunate flint microliths, tanged arrows, and copper awls were the only objects of practical use found.

This burial practice also extended into the Po Plain where in the caves called Buco della Strega and Buco della Sabbia, north of Milan in Lombardy, numbers of winged calcite beads, as well as pendants made from the teeth of a variety of animals have been collected.

Some of the Ligurian caves were used for shelter at this time. Settlement debris in the shape of bucket-shaped pots and carinated vessels were recovered from the Grotta dell'Olivo (Toirano) and similar pottery, including a sherd of Fontbouïsse ware, was found in level 5 at Arene Candide.

The Ligurian coast was thus, at this time, little more than an extension of the cultural scene in southern France and the presence of the Fontbouïsse pottery and winged beads in Remedello contexts further east is made more understandable in the light of these Ligurian finds.

During the Copper Age the Karst caves of the Trieste littoral continue to produce evidence of Central European influence in this small strip of the Adriatic coast line. Fragments of beakers of the Corded Ware culture from Grotta Teresina, decorated with impressions made with a fine cord-wound stick, show us that the East European pastoral migrants who had made their homes in Austria and Slovenia also got as far as the Mediterranean. A larger series of bowls with cruciform feet and cord-impressed or incised geometric designs which are typical products of the Slovenian Ljubljansko Barje culture are also known from the caves of Ciclami, Vlašca and Čotarjova.

BELL BEAKERS

Sherd of bell-shaped beakers with rather stereotyped zone decoration are recorded from a number of Copper Age settlements across the north of Italy, among them Le Colombare, Pescale and the cave of Arma di Nasino in Liguria, while fragments were also found in clearly Early Bronze Age contexts on the Rocca di Rivoli. These sherds and three Beaker burials show us that the Beaker folk, who penetrated almost every corner of Western Europe, were not unknown to the inhabitants of the North Italian Plain. The burials in question have all been found within a few miles of the great Remedello cemetery and they are in fact so near that in the past most prehistorians have regarded them as almost an integral part of the Remedello culture. This is not, however, the case, since an examination of the burial structures and the grave goods shows that these graves have, culturally, little to do with Remedello.

At Ca'di Marco a crouched inhumation in an oval pit had been surrounded by four stout posts, presumably the remains of a mortuary house. With the dead man were the remains of two or three beakers, a black burnished cup with a curvaceous profile and strap handle, two hollow-based arrow-heads of flint, and two lunate microliths. At the nearby site of Santa Cristina two bodies were found side by side in two separate pits and, again, two post-holes were found on one side of them, which may also have been part of a mortuary house structure. In this case one burial had with it a beaker, a flint blade, a tanged copper dagger of traditional Beaker type (so-called Ciempozeulos type), while with the other was a beaker, a trapezoidal copper axe, a boar's tusk and a flint flake. The third Beaker burial of Roccolo Bresciani was from a field adjacent to the Remedello cemetery and was badly disturbed.

Until recently it has generally been assumed that the Beaker people arrived in Northern Italy from Spain, but when one looks closely at the Beaker graves just described the conclusion must be that these people in fact had a Central European origin. The mortuary houses especially are recognizable as a Central European feature with a Corded Ware ancestry, and similarly the Ca'di Marco burnished cup, the hollow-based arrow-head and the tanged dagger are all to be found in Beaker contexts north of the Alps. The Bell Beaker culture itself is, as Neustupný has suggested, in any case more likely to be derived from the Corded Ware cultures of Central Europe than from Spain.

Plate 26

This period of transition between the Neolithic and the full Bronze Age was clearly a time of turmoil and change. Traders and metal prospectors from the eastern Mediterranean may well have sailed up the Po to do business with the inhabitants of Remedello di Sotto and to look for ores in the mountains to the north, while at the same time people from the Fontbouïsse culture from the west, the Bell Beaker tradition from the north, and the Corded Ware culture from the east were all interested in staking their claims on the fringes of the great North Italian Plain.

Contacts with the eastern Mediterranean provide dating evidence for the Remedello metalwork, suggesting that this culture was at its height during the second half of the third millennium B C. Beakers on the other hand, as we shall see, were still in use during the first centuries of the second millennium.

ROCK ART – THE EARLY STAGES

The mountains of Northern Italy possess some of the richest areas of prehistoric rock engravings to be found anywhere in Europe. The finest series lies in the Camonica valley, north of Lake Iseo in Lombardy where, at the small town of Capo di Ponte, Dr E. Anati some years ago set up his centre for the study of prehistoric rock art. Less varied but no less spectacular are the engravings on the remote and desolate mountain slopes of Monte Bego on the Franco-Italian frontier. These were studied in some detail at the turn of the nineteenth century by the retired English clergyman, the Reverend Clarence Bicknell. Other smaller collections of rock engravings have been discovered in Piedmont and in the Veneto at Punta San Virgilio above Lake Garda.

Fig. 29

In almost every case these drawings have been cut or pecked out of the surface of the rocks, which had been polished by the slowly moving ice of Pleistocene glaciers and whose inviting smoothness must have been hard to resist. They are usually found in groups, clustered together on single rock faces or in limited geographical areas. All in all, this rock art clearly covers an extremely long period of time, starting at least as early as the Copper Age and surviving in some instances as late as the nineteenth century.

The motivation which led primitive artists to make these drawings is today not easy to interpret. Much of the earlier art dating to the Copper and Bronze Ages seems to have religious overtones, as we can see in the close relationship between the drawings on rock surfaces in the Val Camonica and the free-standing statue menhirs of the Central Alpine region. The carving on the barren slopes of Monte Bego may well be connected with pilgrimages to some mountain shrine where, on arrival, the devotees would record the event in this manner. The later Iron Age drawings from the Val Camonica, however, appear to have had a more secular character, depicting as they do scenes of everyday life and the heroic exploits of warriors.

Anati has carried out a detailed study of the Val Camonica engravings and has worked out a chronological framework for their whole development. This is based on a detailed study of changes in style and the evidence of superposition of individual drawings as well as on typological comparison of the objects represented in the drawings. As a result, Anati sees the Camunian art as representing a continuous development which started in the Neolithic and evolved through four main phases and many sub-phases, down to the Roman invasion.

For the purpose of this book we will look at the rock art from the Copper and Bronze Age (Anati's period I-III) in this chapter; the Iron Age engravings of the Val Camonica (Anati's phase IV), which have a somewhat different character, will be considered in chapter VIII.

As already mentioned, during the early stages of Camunian art, roughly corresponding to the Copper and Bronze Ages, religious symbolism was strong. Sun discs, praying figures and geometric designs may all be interpreted as cult motifs, while weapons too seem to have had some sort of ritual significance, since they are often represented in large

Plate 28

numbers. Among those depicted during the early period were axes, halberds, and daggers; in fact all the main weapons of the time.

Fig. 30

According to Anati the portrayal of stylized animals starts in the Early Bronze Age along with scenes of hunting and ploughing and other agricultural activities. Also apparently of Bronze Age date are the representations of two- or four-wheeled vehicles, drawings of houses and

Plate 29

field plans.

On Monte Bego there is no evidence to suggest that the tradition of rock art here outlasted the end of the Early Bronze Age and the majority may well date to the Copper Age. There the drawings comprise a less ambitious range of subjects than is found in the Val Camonica, the most usual being scenes of ploughing and representations of men carrying

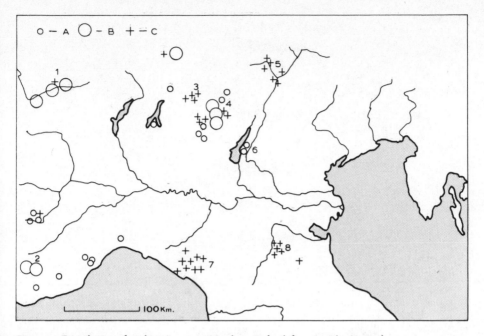

Fig. 29 Distribution of prehistoric art in Northern Italy (after Anati). A Rock engravings; B Large concentrations of rock engravings; C Statue menhirs or anthropomorphic stele. 1 Sion; 2 Monte Bego; 3 Valtellina; 4 Val Camonica; 5 Bolzano-Merano group of stele; 6 Punta San Virgilio; 7 Luni stele; 8 Bologna Iron Age stele

halberds. The stylized heads of oxen, sometimes with enormous ramifications of the horns, are a peculiarity of this group. It is conceivable that there is a tenuous link between these so-called 'bucrania' and the stylized bulls' heads found on the walls of the Sardinian rock-cut tombs of the Copper Age Ozieri culture.

Fig. 31

STATUE MENHIRS

Closely related to the tradition of rock engraving are the schematized human figures known as 'statue menhirs', which have been found in several areas of the Central Alps. There is a group of at least seven figures from the upper valley of the Adige between Bolzano and Merano. Two others have been found in the Val Camonica and seven in the neighbouring Valtellina, a valley to the north-west.

Plate 28

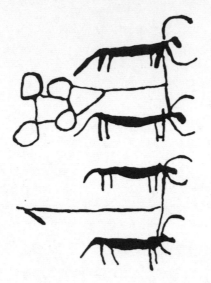

Fig. 30 Engravings from Val Ca-monica. Ox-drawn cart and plough from the Masso di Cemmo no. 2, and houses on the Dos dell'Arca (after Anati)

Fig. 32

The Bolzano-Merano menhirs are headless and only recognizable as human figures by the presence of neck collars in the case of the examples from Termeno and Santa Verena, and by the breasts on the one from Lagundo. The backs of these are often decorated with vertical grooving, representing either hair or a cloak, while most have festoons or multiple lines round their waists which suggest belts. In addition these figures are sometimes provided with axes and daggers and the representation of a four-wheeled wagon was carved on the lower part of the figure B from Lagundo.

The Valtellina menhirs differ from the others in that, where the head should be, they have a rayed disc, which could well be interpreted as a solar symbol. Some of the menhirs in this group also have impressions of feet, and wagons carved on them.

Whether these primitive stone statues are monuments to dead ancestors or served to represent some deity, a sun god in the case of the Valtellina figures or possibly a fertility goddess in the case of Lagundo, it is unfortunately impossible to say with any degree of certainty.

Similar standing figures are known in several parts of the western Mediterranean. The nearest and probably the most pertinent parallels to the North Italian series are the examples from Lébous in Provence and Sion in the Upper Rhône valley which are both Copper Age in date,

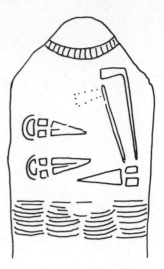

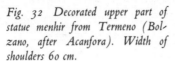

Fig. 31 Ligurian rock engravings. Man with large halberd from Monte Bego, and schematized bulls' heads (bucrania) (after Bicknell)

Fig. 32 Decorated upper part of statue menhir from Termeno (Bolzano, after Acanfora). Width of shoulders 60 cm.

and both of which occur in association with cultures (Fontbouïsse in the case of Lébous and Beaker at Sion) that had some connection with Northern Italy. However, comparisons can also be made with figures from Corsica and the Lunigana region of northern Tuscany which, to judge from their swords, can hardly be older than the Middle Bronze Age.

In the past, speculation as to the dating of these Bolzano-Merano figures has ranged from the Copper Age to the Iron Age without any firm conclusions being reached. However, the evidence recently assembled by Anati clearly suggests that these monuments were put up during the Copper and Early Bronze Ages, a conclusion which is supported by the discovery at Sion, where a 'statue menhir' decorated with a dagger identical to examples found on the Bolzano-Merano menhirs, had been re-used as a walling slab in a Bell Beaker cist burial.

CHAPTER V

The Polada Culture and other Early Bronze Age Communities (c. 1800–1450 BC)

As early as 1800 BC the first full Bronze Age settlements had been established around the Northern Plain. These Early Bronze Age peoples now had a good technological knowledge of making bronze implements, even though they still used flint for making sickles, saws and arrow-heads.

POLADA

Fig. 33

The only tradition that can be well defined in our area during the Early Bronze Age is found in the large series of settlements scattered along the southern fringe of the Alps from Piedmont in the west to the head of the Adriatic in the east. These sites together make up the Polada culture, which, owing to the remarkable preservation of finds from many of its settlements can claim to be one of the most fully documented cultures in the prehistory of Europe. It is one of those curious paradoxes that we find so often in archaeology, that whereas our knowledge of the Copper Age came almost entirely from cemeteries, evidence for the Polada people is derived almost exclusively from settlement sites.

The types of sites chosen for Polada villages were extremely varied and are in many respects comparable with those of the Neolithic period, from which there was undoubtedly some direct line of descent. Thus we find settlements in valleys, on the plain, on hill-tops and some even in caves. The most distinctive sites, however, are the lake villages. A remarkable number of these lake-side settlements were built during this period and it is these, with their waterlogged deposits, that have preserved a wealth of organic remains of the kind usually completely absent on dry land sites.

Lake villages are especially well represented around the small lakes and peat bogs that formed in the poorly drained basins of the end-moraine of lake Garda and the lakes of Lombardy and Piedmont. In the Garda moraine we find the type site of Polada itself, as well as other important settlements such as Barche di Solferino, Cattaragna and Lucone.

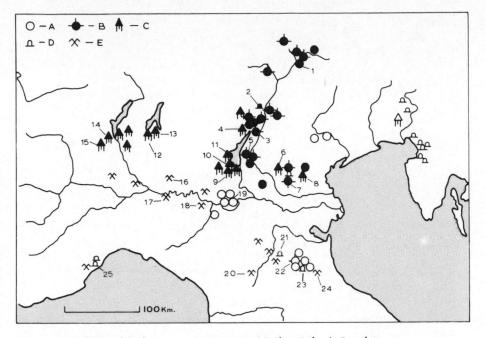

Fig. 33 Distribution of Early Bronze Age remains in Northern Italy. A Low-lying open settlement; B Hill settlement; C Lake village; D Cave settlement; E Hoard of metalwork. Polada sites are shown in black. 1 Plabach; 2 La Vela; 3 Mori; 4 Ledro; 5 Rocca di Rivoli; 6 Fimon; 7 Monte Tondo; 8 Arquà; 9 Barche di Solferino; 10 Polada; 11 Lucone; 12 Isola dei Cipressi; 13 Bosisio; 14 Gagnano; 15 Mercurago; 16 Lodi; 17 Castel S. Giovanni; 18 Castione; 19 Lagazzi; 20 Burzanella; 21 Grotta Farneto; 22 Monte Castelaccio, Imola; 23 Tanaccia di Brisighella; 24 S. Lorenzo Noceto; 25 Arene Candide

Among comparable villages are, from west to east, Mercurago in Piedmont, Pusiano in Lombardy (with its settlements, on the Isola dei Cipressi and at Bosisio), Ledro north of Garda, and also three sites on Lake Fimon and one at Arquà in the Euganean Hills of the Veneto. It is very apparent that the shores of the larger lakes like Maggiore, Como, and Garda were avoided at this time, although villages of later Bronze Age date are found along their shores.

Many of these lake villages have been partially excavated, but by far the most productive excavations have been those by F. Zorzi at Barche di Solferino in 1939 and the work carried out by R. Battaglia and others at Molina, on the small mountain lake of Ledro, high above the north-western end of Lake Garda.

Both the location and the details of construction and the economy of these lake villages point to a direct derivation from the Neolithic lakeside settlements discussed on p. oo, although only at Lagozza does there appear to be any actual continuity of occupation from Neolithic to Bronze Age times. Many of these villages were built on artificial plat-forms, of horizontally laid criss-cross timbers and brushwood intended to protect the houses from flood or damp, and the settlements of Barche di Solferino and Arquà provide good examples of these so-called *bonifica* constructions. The forest of piles in the shore of the Lake Molina di Ledro suggests another type of construction. It is still a matter of some argument as to whether this village was built on a platform supported by piles over the water, as Battaglia originally supposed, or whether the posts were just the remains of house structures or successive breakwaters and piles put in to strengthen the steep bank of the lake shore. A flooring of regularly laid planks was in fact found on the landward side of the settlement in the excavations carried out by Battaglia between 1927 and 1937 which suggests that at least part of this site was constructed *bonifica* fashion at ground level; but it is possible, on the other hand, that the buildings fronting the lake may have projected out over the water, in the manner of fishermen's huts still to be seen along the Adriatic today.

Some of the timbers at Ledro have horizontal beams slotted into them to form part of a rigid construction. Other posts are re-used house timbers, like the one with a series of mortice slots cut into it which may have originally been a sleeper beam holding upright plank walling. Nothing to suggest the actual outlines of the houses was preserved at Ledro or any other site, although from the structural fragments we might conclude that they were rectangular.

The Polada hill settlements were often strategically sited and we find for example that the summit of the Rocca di Rivoli, dominating the Adige trade route at the northern end of the Chiusa gorge, was re-occupied at this time. Another village with a good commanding position was the Colle di San Bartolomeo, in the Sarca plain north of Lake Garda. Here the excavator noted traces of a four-foot-wide rampart of dry stone walling from the Early Bronze Age occupation.

Plate 30

Plate 31

Plate 33

Fig. 34, d

In a settlement on top of Monte Tondo in the Berici Hills, the upper hill slope had been terraced for the construction of houses, while lower terraces were probably used for cultivation. We may have here the earliest evidence in Italy of terrace cultivation, which is still such a characteristic feature of the Mediterranean landscape.

The only burials that can be attributed to the Polada culture are a small number from natural rock shelters along the Adige Valley in the province of Trento. One of these, an inhumation burial at Colombo di Mori, near Rovereto, was discovered in a small cave set in a cliff immediately below a Polada hill village. Another recently excavated rock shelter at Vela near Trento contained the grave of a man buried beneath a cairn of stones. He was accompanied by a group of Polada pots and a necklace composed of several hundred beads made from twisted copper wire, marble, *dentalium* shell, and animal teeth. Immediately below the burial the floor of a bronze worker's furnace was revealed, surrounded by piles of bronze slag and ingots. It is rather tempting to see the burial as that of the same smith who had set up his business in this rock hollow.

Fig. 34 Polada wooden objects from Ledro: a cup with cut-out decoration; b rough-out for cup; c churn; d beam with mortice holes; e saw with flint teeth (a–c, e after Battaglia; d after Tomasi). b 6 cm. diameter; c 21 cm. diameter; d 30.5 cm. high; e approx. 31 cm. long

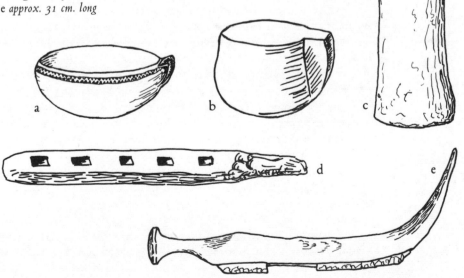

Plate 34

The economy of the Polada culture is especially well documented in the waterlogged sites of Molina di Ledro and Barche. Their agricultural activities included the growing of einkorn and emmer wheat, barley and flax, the latter probably having been cultivated both for its oil and for weaving thread. Farm implements have also survived. At Ledro, Battaglia found a well preserved wooden crook-ard, which has a good claim to be the earliest surviving plough so far discovered in Europe. From Barche there is a wooden sickle shaped rather like a jaw-bone with a cutting edge of inserted flints, a type of implement which was used by the first farmers of the Near East. A number of rather similar well-made tools with flint cutting edges from Ledro can be interpreted as saws or rasps, rather than as sickles, since the cutting edges are set into the outside of the wooden haft.

As with the Neolithic lake dwellers before them, agriculture was by no means the Polada people's only source of vegetable food, as we can conclude from the large quantities of different wild fruits and nuts that have survived in the lake settlements. At Ledro thick layers of stones of the wild Cornel cherry extended right across parts of the settlement, and there were similar accumulations of berry pips from Barche and Pascalone (Fimon). Harvests such as these must surely be connected with the making of wine or a similar beverage. Acorns formed another staple of diet and were probably used for flour. Direct evidence for the process, known from ethnographic sources, of roasting acorns prior to grinding in order to extract their bitter flavour, was provided at Pascalone (Fimon) where burnt acorns were found in a pot. In addition wild apples, plums, strawberries, raspberries, elderberries and grapes were collected, and beech mast and hazel nuts are represented as well.

The inhabitants of the Early Bronze Age lake village on Fimon made use of the water chestnut just like the Neolithic inhabitants at the neighbouring, but far more ancient site of Molino Casarotto.

A burnt hemispherical mass, which may have been a loaf of bread, was also found at Ledro, and carbonized balls of a similar consistency, which strangely resemble the present-day *pasta* speciality of the Veneto known as *gnocchi*.

Among the domestic animals, cattle, sheep, pig and horse are all found and there is some evidence that butter and cheese were made. At Ledro, recently discovered long, narrow 'churns' made from a hollowed tree

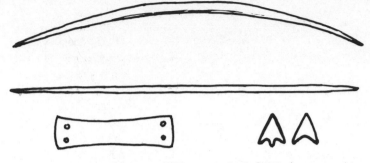

Fig. 35   Archery equipment. Bows and flint arrow-heads from Ledro; stone wristguard from Polada (after Battaglia). Bows 1.44 m. and 1.07 m. long

trunk with a short handle tab on the rim are strikingly like modern stave churns still used in many parts of Europe. A wooden whisk from Barche and conical pottery sieves from Ledro of the type known already to the Neolithic inhabitants of Lagozza and Rivoli may well be connected with the boiling of milk or the manufacture of cheese.

The bones of wild animals again feature prominently in all Polada excavations and at Arquà and Pascalone (Fimon) almost all the fauna was wild. Red deer and roe deer and wild boar are the most common game, but brown bear and beaver, which were presumably hunted for their skins, are represented as well.

The bow and arrow which had gone out of fashion by the Early Bronze Age in many areas north of the Alps, were retained by the Polada people as their main weapons for hunting and warfare. This archery equipment – small triangular barbed and tanged and hollow-based flint arrow-heads, as well as rectangular stone wrist guards – is very reminiscent of that used by the Bell Beaker culture. On the other hand, triangular transverse arrow-heads may well have a local Lagozza culture ancestry. Several wooden bows varying in length between 2 foot 3½ inches and 4 foot 8½ inches were found at Ledro, and an arrow with a heavy wooden head, presumably used for stunning birds and small game, was preserved at Barche. A spring-loaded wooden game-trap came to light during peat-digging operations in the Fimon basin in the nineteenth century. Although its date is probably Early Bronze Age, it could possibly be earlier.

Fishing must have been an important source of food in these settlements, although actual fish bones are recorded only from a few sites.

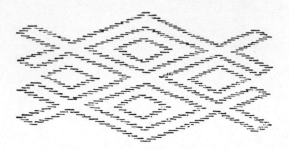

Fig. 36 Embroidered cloth from Ledro (after Perini). Actual size

Fig. 38 Polada metalwork. Ring ingot, axe from Torbole (Trento) and pins from Ledro

Pike for example is recorded from Pascalone (Fimon) along with the shells of a large number of freshwater turtles. Wooden floats from fishing nets and the remains of fish weirs were discovered beneath three feet of peat at Gagnano (Piedmont) and may be connected with a nearby Bronze Age settlement.

Polada settlements provide us with the earliest evidence for wheeled vehicles in Italy. At Barche, Zorzi recovered a model spoked wheel which must be one of the earliest examples of its type in Europe. Two full size wheels, one solid and made up of three planks and the other spoked, were found at Mercurago (Piedmont), but it is not now possible to tell whether these belong to the Early or the Middle Bronze Age phase of settlement on that site.

Fig. 37

Plate 36

Dug out canoes have been found in many of the excavated lake settlements as, for example, at Barche, Ledro and Pascalone (Fimon). An exceptionally fine specimen, fashioned from the trunk of an oak and with a carved prow pierced for mooring, has recently been brought to light at the lake settlement of Lucone (Brescia).

Spindle whorls and loom weights are common on most sites, and at Ledro fragments of fine linen textiles and balls of flax thread were preserved. Some of this cloth bears the traces of woven patterns. One very long narrow strip, perhaps a belt, was embroidered at either end with panels of intersecting lines and lozenges, while another scrap had small seeds stitched onto it for ornament.

The inhabitants of the Polada settlements immediately to the north of Lake Garda were competent bronze workers and in fact the Polada culture has the most advanced metal technology of any Early Bronze Age culture in Italy. Moulds, crucibles, and conical clay nozzles for bellows are known from Ledro and other sites in the province of Trento

Fig. 37 Wooden wheels from the settlement at Mercurago (Piedmont)

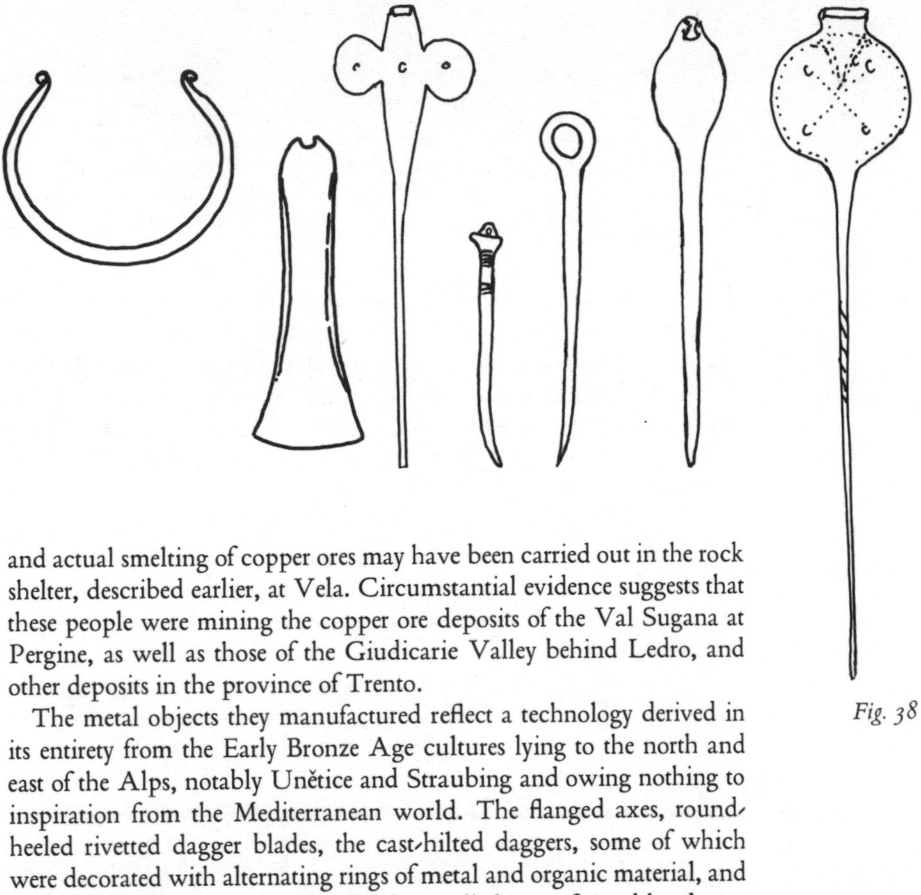

and actual smelting of copper ores may have been carried out in the rock shelter, described earlier, at Vela. Circumstantial evidence suggests that these people were mining the copper ore deposits of the Val Sugana at Pergine, as well as those of the Giudicarie Valley behind Ledro, and other deposits in the province of Trento.

The metal objects they manufactured reflect a technology derived in its entirety from the Early Bronze Age cultures lying to the north and east of the Alps, notably Unětice and Straubing and owing nothing to inspiration from the Mediterranean world. The flanged axes, round-heeled rivetted dagger blades, the cast-hilted daggers, some of which were decorated with alternating rings of metal and organic material, and the various pins with flat decorated disc, rolled or perforated heads, are all types closely paralleled north of the Alps. Metal objects are, however, rare in the Polada settlements to the west and east of the Adige, where flint was still the main raw material for the manufacture of blade tools.

Fig. 38

Pottery is abundant on the lake sites, where pots frequently escaped breakage. No less than 480 complete pots were recovered during Zorzi's short season of excavations at Barche and far more must have come out over the years from the Molina site at Ledro.

Pot forms are for the most part fairly standard and purely functional. Characteristic are the large, deep, single-handled cups with sinuous profile and the wide bowls with rounded or carinated profile, all in fine

Plate 32

75

Fig. 39

burnished dark-surfaced ware. Flat-bottomed, one-handled conical cups and large bucket- or barrel-shaped cooking or storage vessels with two handles and cordon decoration are of coarser ware.

Handles are plugged into the pot wall and consist either of a simple strap or else a strap bent in the middle to form an elbow. The latter is a very distinctive feature of Polada ceramics, although it should be remembered that it is a type of handle which was widely used during the Copper Age in Southern Italy, and in the North in the Remedello culture.

Apart from cordons on the coarser pottery, other forms of pottery decoration are rare, although there is a group of bowls from Barche with elaborate cruciform designs incised on their bases. These designs remind one rather of decoration found on Jugoslav Vučedol pottery of an only slightly earlier date. On the other hand, the 'bent corn' motif found on some vessels, is paralleled among the repertoire of pot decoration that was in vogue in the roughly contemporary Castelluccio culture in Sicily.

The Barche bowls show that regional variation did exist within the pottery tradition of the Polada culture, and another local style is represented at Arquà in the Euganean hills where polypod bowls, perhaps with a Beaker culture ancestry, are a common type of vessel.

Wooden bowls with elbow handles, often still in an unfinished state, are found on a number of the waterlogged sites. One wooden bowl from Ledro is decorated with a band of reserve zig-zags incised with the *Kerbschnitt* technique. As we saw before, this characteristic method of decorating wooden objects was sometimes applied to pottery, as in the Neolithic at Chiozza, but in the Polada culture it was a technique used only in the decoration of woodwork.

Fig. 34, b

The Polada people made a variety of personal ornaments including 'v' perforated buttons of bone and a large assortment of beads and

Fig. 39 Characteristic forms of Polada pottery. Above, 'bent corn' motif on sherd from Polada (after Munro); below, pottery from Ledro (after Tomasi)

pendants. Besides the varieties of beads already described in the Vela burial, there are the remains of a fine necklace of limestone and glass frit beads from the lake village of Lucone and amber beads from Ledro. The teeth of bear and boar and, at Ledro, even bear jaws – all trophies of the hunt – were also perforated for use as pendants.

Plate 35

The Polada culture in the Adige valley became especially prosperous not only on the local mineral wealth, but also probably because this valley leads north to the Central Alpine passes. We can assume that it was along this valley that trade passed between Northern and Central Europe and the Mediterranean, and the metalwork has shown us how closely Polada was linked with the Straubing and Unětice culture north of the Alps. It is probable that copper ring ingots of Unětice type from the Adige valley, and those associated with flat axes in the hoard found at Lodi in Lombardy, are the tangible remains of a metal trade between Central Europe and the south. The amber beads from Molino di Ledro certainly came over the Alps from the distant Baltic.

There is some indirect evidence of contacts with Mycenaean Greece. For example at Ledro a local potter made a convincing copy of a metal Mycenaean Vapheio-type cup with its distinctive flaring outline and loop handle on the rim. The spoked wheel from Barche, the earliest in Europe outside Greece, could likewise be of southern European inspiration.

Important evidence of Early Bronze Age inter-tribal contact is the series of little fired clay plaques, known from a number of Polada settlements in the Garda area. These were adorned before firing with horizontal lines, along which a variety of symbols had been carefully impressed with fine, especially prepared, stamps. These symbols include concentric circles of different dimensions, arrangements of three or six dots in triangles or rectangles, and other simple marks. The rather abacus-like appearance of the general design and the numerical character of the stamps suggests that they might have been a sort of counting device. Could these have been talleys, perhaps used in trading? Such a hypothesis receives support from the discovery of identical plaques in the Mad'arovce culture of Slovakia and on contemporary sites in Hungary, both dating to the final phase of the Early Bronze Age (Reinecke A2). We might also wonder whether they may not have been inspired in some way by Mycenaean clay tablets?

Fig. 40

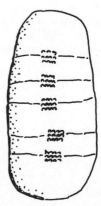

Fig. 40   Plaque of fired clay with linear and impressed dot motifs from Cattaragna (Brescia)

As regards the chronology of the Polada culture L. Fasani has recently suggested that there were two phases of development. An early horizon (Polada A) is clearly represented at Barche and can be correlated with Reinecke's A1 stage of metalworking north of the Alps (1800–1550 BC). Its early date is confirmed too by the association of Barche-style Polada pottery with sherds of bell-beakers on the Rocca di Rivoli. The main floruit of the Polada culture on sites like Ledro and Lucone is during Fasani's phase B (*c.* 1550–1450 BC) which is characterized by the more abundant Reinecke A2 style metal products. Carbon 14 dates for Polada are rather inconsistent, varying from 1709± 105 to 1187± 105 BC at Ledro, and 1545±60 BC from Cavriana, to cite a few.

We have seen that the elements that made up the Polada culture are very varied in origin. Metallurgy from Central Europe, elements of pottery design from the South Italian Copper Age, hunting equipment from the Beaker culture are all there; but probably the most significant is the unmistakable survival of local settlement patterns and economy from earlier Neolithic times.

THE EARLY BRONZE AGE ELSEWHERE IN THE NORTH

It is difficult to draw the geographical boundaries of the Polada culture, since, when we move away from the stretch of the southern group fringe of the Alps between Piedmont and the Veneto, evidence of Early Bronze Age settlement dwindles. To the east, some of the caves in the Julian Alps (Velika Jama) and on the Trieste Karst (Grotta dei Ciclami) have levels containing pottery with elbow handles which remind one of Polada, but there are also two-handled hour-glass beakers very similar to the drinking vessels of the Austrian Early Bronze Age culture of Wieselburg.

High up in the mountains towards the Central Alpine passes is a variant of Polada, the Plabach or Rivapiana group, known from a number of hill-top settlements in the area of Bressanone. Among these sites is the promontory fort of Nosingbühel, just north of Bressanone, which has a stone rampart on its landward side. The Tyrolean anti-quarian Eggers, moreover, claimed to have found hearths and hut foundations at Plabach itself.

In the centre of the North Italian plain between Cremona and Mantua, in low-lying marshy terrain not far from the River Po itself, there are two

Fig. 41 Lagazzi di Vhò. Section through a series of Early Bronze Age huts |_____| **2 m.**

sites, Lagazzi di Vhò and Cella Dati, which could be regarded as outlying settlements of the Polada culture. At Lagazzi some eight low circular mounds were visible at ground level before excavation. These varied between 15 and 18 feet in diameter and proved to consist of a succession of superimposed hut floors and hearths which had been built up periodically to raise the site above the flood level. They remind one strongly of the hearth at Molino Casarotto. The finds from these sites are very like those from the Polada settlements, although axe handles and double perforated lugs on the pottery suggest that we are again dealing with a regional style Bernabò Brea called the Lagazzi tradition. Lagazzi produced a unique example of a 'v' perforated button made of amber, an object otherwise only known from Early Bronze Age Denmark and Britain. Lagazzi type axe handles also feature in the Lombard Lake settlement of Mercurago, and in Liguria.

Fig. 41

Fig. 42

A glance at the map will show that in southern Lombardy and south of the Po, Early Bronze Age settlements are few and far between, apart from a group of sites in the Imola and Faenza districts. Perhaps some of the Terremare settlements started during this period but this is certainly difficult to demonstrate.

Curiously enough these parts of Lombardy and Emilia, so devoid of settlements, have produced a notable series of hoards of Early Bronze Age bronze implements. Most of these (*e.g.* Baragello, Burzanella, Sasso Marconi, Savignano) are made up of flanged axes, with as many as 96 in the Savignano hoard. Others show more variety, like the find made as long ago as 1694 at S. Noceto (Forli), with 5 or 6 daggers, some ingot torques and 41 axes. The Lodi (Lombardy) hoard too had 16 axes and 6 ring ingots, while at Castione and Castel San Giovanni only cast-hilted daggers were found.

Plate 37

All these objects, like the Polada metalwork, are in the style of contemporary Central European technology. Further south, however, in the territory of the Early Apennine culture this northern influence fades away.

Of the small group of sites with Early Bronze Age occupation south of the Po, a number are inhabited caves. In the small Tanaccia di Brisighella, recently excavated by Scarani, material was recovered which gives the impression of a transitional stage between the Copper and the Early Bronze Age. Elbow handles feature on the pottery and the decoration of one vessel appears to be influenced by late Bell Beaker pottery. The cave of Farneto in the Apennine foot-hills behind Bologna is probably slightly later in date, having bowls with axe-shaped append-ages on their handles as well as some rather unusual scratched decoration on the pottery.

Then there is the Monte Castellaccio, a naturally defended hill projecting out onto the Plain at Imola. This site was masterfully excavated by Scarabelli between 1873 and 1883. He found several roughly circular post settings for huts averaging about 15 feet in diameter which were, in some cases, associated with clay hearths. There were also a number of pits dug into the subsoil, whose use as storage silos was demonstrated by a quantity of burnt wheat found lying in the bottom of one of them. The finds from Monte Castellaccio suggest an occupation both during the Early and the Middle Bronze Age. Tanged and oval flint arrow-heads, flint sickle blades and perforated flat-iron axes of polished hard stone were widely used in the Early Bronze Age phase and fine black burnished plain carinated bowls with roll-ended tab handles and double perforated lugs probably also belong to the early period of occupation. Among the domesticated animals there was a predominance of cattle over horse, sheep or goat and pig, while hunting and collecting was as important here as it was north of Po with red deer second only to cattle. Other wild foods included duck, freshwater mussels and acorns. A hint of canni-balism is perhaps to be seen in the human bones scattered among settlement debris, although other explanations could probably be found.

Little is known about the Early Bronze Age on the Ligurian coast, the finds being restricted to a hoard of flat axes from Rocca delle Fene and a few potsherds, including axe handles and fragments with incised motifs from the caves of Arene Candide and Pollera. Continuing further west along the same coast line to the Rhône Valley we meet with other cave settlements characterized by pottery with elbow handles which may in some way be distantly related to Polada.

Fig. 42   Lagazzi di Vhò. 'v' perforated amber button. Actual size

CHAPTER VI

The Middle and Late Bronze Age
(1450–1100 BC)

For the two and a half centuries following the breakdown of the Polada tradition, new cultures emerged on the North Italian Plain whose origins were clearly rooted in Polada. The metal technology of these people was still heavily dependent on new developments in the lands to the north and east of the Alps which continued as before to be the industrial heart of Europe. Sometimes these contacts with Central Europe became so intense that the archaeological evidence might well be interpreted in terms of an actual invasion or at least political and economic domination of the Po Valley by people from the east.

The prosperity of the settlements in the Po Valley, with their extensive use of Central European-style metalwork, continues to contrast with the conservative and technologically more backward communities of Central and Southern Italy, for to the south the Apennine Bronze Age which made its first appearance sometime about 1800 BC lived on almost unchanged till the very end of the second millennium. Practising an economy based on mixed agriculture and pastoralism, these Apennine Bronze Age peoples had little interest in exploiting their own metal resources.

The period of time we have chosen in this chapter, lasting from about 1450 to 1100 and corresponding approximately to Reinecke's B and D phases of metalwork north of the Alps, is conventionally called the Middle and Late Bronze Age even though the differences between these two stages are not, as far as North Italy is concerned, culturally very significant.

From about 1450 onwards three quite distinct settlement areas are recognizable on the Plain centred on the regions of the Veneto, Emilia and Lombardy. It is probably no coincidence that these cover almost exactly the same territories as do the later three main Iron Age civilizations of the north.

It is only round the shores of Lake Garda, thanks mainly to the studies of L. Fasani and A. Aspes, that we have any clear idea of the sequence of development of the Middle and Late Bronze Age in the Veneto. Three phases have now been recognized. Earliest is the Bor phase, characterized by metalwork of Reinecke B type (1450–1300 BC). Following this are the stages of Isolone (1300–1250 BC) and Peschiera (1250–1100 BC) with mainly Reinecke D style metal equipment. Each of these phases takes its name from a settlement site, all three of which are lake or river-side villages.

Although many Polada settlements had been abandoned, some characteristic lake sites such as Lucone, Bande di Cavriana and Ledro continued to be occupied during the Bor phase. New waterside locations were, however, chosen for villages and for the first time settlements appear on the shores of the larger lakes including Garda itself. Bor di Pacengo was one of these new villages and here, as at the nearby contemporary settlement of Cisano, wooden piles have been located off-shore just below the surface of the water.

Not far away at the foot of Lake Garda, where the River Mincio flows out of the lake, lies Peschiera. This Bronze Age settlement was dis-covered in 1860 during dredging operations in the harbour of the (then) Austrian fortress. This and subsequent work in the harbour produced more than 2,000 articles of bronze, bone objects, and pottery, from among the charred piles of the village which once lay astride the foot of the lake.

Fig. 46

Villages on Garda have the disadvantage of being still submerged below the level of the lake, so that all the archaeological discoveries so far made have been rather rudely snatched from the lake bed by means of grabs and dredges, a procedure which provides little information about settlement plan or stratigraphy.

One site which was more suitable for excavation was Isolone on an island in the River Mincio only a few miles down-stream from Peschiera. On excavation the site, a veritable forest of piles, was found to cover an area measuring some 300× 100 yards.

The economy of these sites was not very different from that of the Polada culture and even in the latest of these villages, Peschiera, a mixture of wild and domesticated animals is represented along with wild vegetable remains.

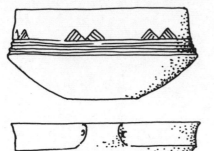

Fig. 43   Pottery and metalwork of the Middle Bronze Age from Bor di Pacengo on Lake Garda; top right, pelta motif on pottery

The Bor settlement, as Aspes and Fasani have recently shown, is of special importance as it was only occupied for a short period of time. Unfortunately the same cannot be said of the later type sites of Isolone and Peschiera.

The bronzes from Bor are all of one period and comparable with Reinecke's phase B metalwork north of the Alps. Evidence of the new mode of warfare using the sword and the spear, which spread across most of Central Europe shortly after 1450 BC, is also found at Bor as well as elsewhere in the Po Plain this time. Other equipment now made for the first time in bronze includes arrow-heads and sickles, although indeed the same objects made in flint still outnumber those in bronze in this settlement.

Daggers with trapezoidal and triangular rivetted heel-plates are characteristic of this phase, replacing the Early Bronze Age forms with semicircular heels. These new dagger blades now also have a lozenge-shaped cross-section which gives them greater strength. Axes too have an improved hafting, being provided with high cast medial wings. There are also new pins such as the triple ring-headed pin and the 'toggle' pin, which has a flat head and a swollen neck perforated to take a securing thong. Metal buttons, pendants, and combs are other novelties.

Metal products belonging to the initial stages of the Late Bronze Age were found at Isolone, but far more interesting is the great collection of

Fig. 43

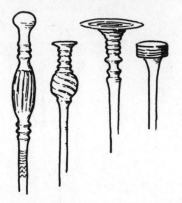

Fig. 44 Late Bronze Age pins from Peschiera

bronzes from the village of Peschiera. Here, besides metal objects similar to those from Bor such as trapezoidal rivetted heeled daggers, we find later-style flange-hilted daggers with long rivetted tangs. There are also hump-backed ring-handled knives, double-edged razors, and hundreds of pins with all manner of globular, disc, biconical, vase and wound-wire heads. Most of this material can be paralleled in Reinecke's phase D north of the Alps.

Figs. 44, 45

The earliest type of fibula is also represented here: the so-called violin-bow or Peschiera fibula. This has a flat twisted-wire bow and a simple catch plate, and is the earliest type of spring safety-pin to be found in Europe – it was probably invented somewhere between Lake Garda and the Austrian Alps round about 1250 B C.

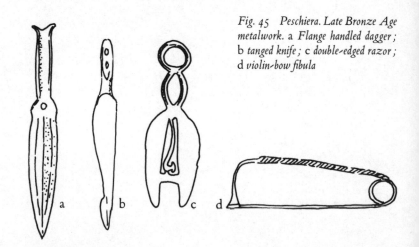

Fig. 45 Peschiera. Late Bronze Age metalwork. a Flange handled dagger; b tanged knife; c double-edged razor; d violin-bow fibula

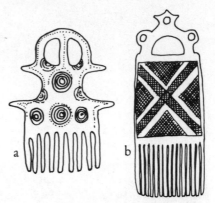

Fig. 46 Combs from Peschiera:
a *metal;* b *bone*

The Middle and Late Bronze Age pottery styles of the Garda region are best seen in the collections from Bor and Isolone. Among the Bor pottery we can recognize Polada forms like the bag-shaped cups with one handle, but the trend now is for wide bowls with sharp carinations. Horned handles replace the earlier elbow ones and flattened bobbin-type lugs are usual. New is the grooved decoration, used in multilinear bands, semicircles, and hatched triangles; and grooved designs are found on the bottoms of pots as well. Some of these innovations in the design and decorations of pottery find remarkably close parallels in Hungary. Not only are there bosses and grooved decoration, but one bowl from Bor decorated with a complicated pelta-shaped grooved design has its exact counterpart in the Central Danubian Plain.

Fig. 43
Fig. 47, a

Fig. 43

In the eastern Veneto near Vicenza and Padua the Middle Bronze Age sites are poorer in metal, and pottery styles differ from those found on Lake Garda. Although the occupation of some settlements continues through from the Early Bronze Age (Arquà and Monte Tondo) many of the sites were new foundations like Castellon del Brosimo, a hill settlement in the Berici Hills to the north of Monte Tondo, and the large village of Marendole in the Plain near Padua.

On Lake Fimon a new lake village was built at the Ponte del Debba not very far from the Early Bronze Age site of Pascalone, and it is interesting to see that the largely wild fauna of the older site had now been replaced by domesticated animals. The complete abandonment of lake settlements by the end of the second millennium – Peschiera being one of the last – is probably closely related to a shift from a mixed economy of hunting and agriculture to one based entirely on farming.

Fig. 47

While some of the pottery and the horned handles found in the eastern Veneto are comparable to those found on the Garda sites, the keeled and cylindrical appendages on other handles are a local feature. Both types are reminiscent of bowl handles found in south-east Emilia and may reflect the presence of direct cultural connections across the eastern end of the Po Plain.

High up the Adige and Isarco valleys the inhabitants of the hill settlements of the Plabach (Rivapiana) culture continued to be occupied, the coarse pottery found in them differing little from that of the Early Bronze Age apart from a concession to the Middle Bronze Age fashion of horned handles.

Fig. 48

During the Middle and Late Bronze Age, settlements encroached further into the Plain and these in turn were in contact with the northerly Terremare settlements on the Po. On the Plain to the south of Verona

Fig. 47 Bowl handles. a Horned handle of Garda area; b Pillar and keeled handles of eastern Veneto; c Terremare handles of western Emilia; d Terremare handles of eastern Emilia

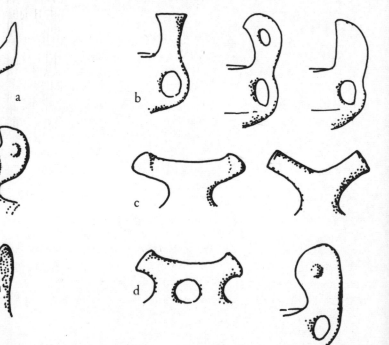

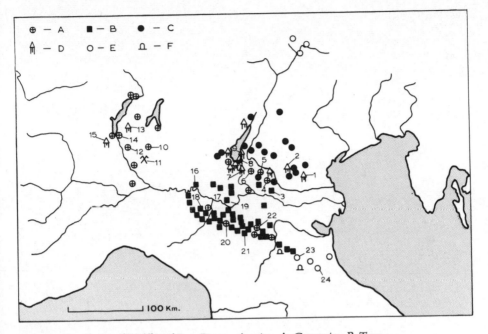

Fig. 48 Distribution of Middle and Late Bronze Age sites. A Cemeteries; B Terre-mare settlements; C Open settlements of the Venetic Bronze Age; D Lake settlements; E Other open sites; F Cave settlements; 1 Arquà; 2 Fimon; 3 Castel del Tartaro; 4 Bovolone; 5 Povegliano; 6 Franzine; 7 Isolone; 8 Peschiera; 9 Bor di Pacengo; 10 Monza; 11 Cascina Ranza; 12 Canegrate; 13 Bodio; 14 Coarezzo; 15 Mercurago; 16 Santa Cristina; 17 Gottolengo; 18 Castione; 19 Zaffenella; 20 Montata; 21 Gorzano; 22 Casinalbo; 23 Monte Castellaccio; 24 Bertarina

are a number of cemeteries belonging to this period. At Povegliano Veronese extended inhumation burials were found associated with cremations, the earliest evidence of this burial rite in Northern Italy. Five of the Povegliano inhumations were accompanied by swords while others had rivetted daggers. Pins with triple ring heads and even more elaborate ring-headed pins, as well as 'toggle' pins, amber beads and a few flint artifacts complete the list of grave goods.

The same mixed burial rite has been found in a slightly later cemetery at Franzine where one supine female inhumation was provided with spiral wound-wire ear-rings and an enormous pair of globular-headed

Fig. 49   Urn from the Middle Bronze Age
cremation cemetery at Bovolone (Verona)

Fig. 50 Middle Bronze Age swords.
a Terremare type from Ostiglia; b Sauerbrunn type from Salgareda; c, d Lombard
swords related to the Rixheim tradition. 1 : 5

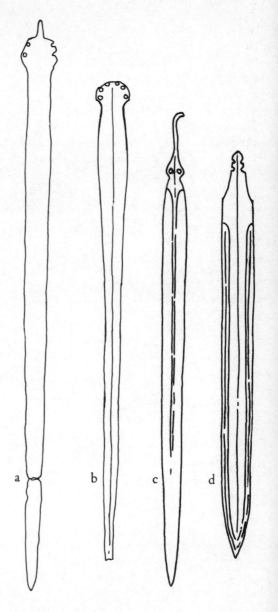

pins on each shoulder for dress fastening. The cremations from Franzine
and another nearby cemetery, Bovolone, were contained in globular
urns which usually have a pair of vertical cylindrical sleeve handles on
the shoulders. They are either plain or are provided with wide grooved
decoration.

Fig. 49

From a study of the associated bronzes, Povegliano can be roughly
equated with the fourteenth-century B C Bor settlement, Franzine; and
Bovolone with the Isolone and Peschiera periods of the thirteenth/twelfth
centuries. (Reinecke D or even the start of Halstatt A1).

These burials throw further light on the connections between the
Veneto and Central Europe. Supine inhumations and cremations as
well as sword burials are all found in the Middle Bronze Age in
Hungary. The dress fashion with two large shoulder pins, used in
exactly the same way as at Franzine, is likewise a feature of Hungarian
Middle Bronze Age burials.

Furthermore, there are the swords found at Povegliano, for these too
belong to the Hungarian types classified by Cowen as Sauerbrunn, Boiu
and Smolnice. Cowen and Foltiny's studies of the bronze swords of
Southern Europe show that there was an almost continuous distribution
of these classes of swords from the Veneto eastwards across the Julian
Alps through to Hungary and Bohemia.

As Cowen has pointed out, these swords are graphic evidence of the
experimental stages in the development of the earliest European swords.
The Sauerbrunn sword, the earliest of the series, was not at all an
efficient weapon, being no more than an elongated version of the Early
Bronze Age dagger with a rounded rivetted heel. Like those daggers
too it was decorated with incised patterns on the blade. The fact that
many of these Sauerbrunn swords have torn rivet holes shows that their
weakness lay in their hafting, the heavy blade causing too much strain
to the rivets. In the later Boiu-type swords, short tangs projecting from
the heel were added in an attempt to remedy this fault. Even more
satisfactory hafting methods, using flanged hilts or hilts cast solid with
the blade, were also being experimented with in Central Europe. These
types, however, are rare in the Veneto, the only example being one of the
Smolnice type from Povegliano.

Fig. 50

All these three sword types accompanied burials at Povegliano while
no less than 16 similar examples have also been found in the gravels of

the three rivers, Sile, Piave and Livenza, which flow through the province of Treviso into the Adriatic just north of Venice. So large a quantity of swords and other bronze work as has been recovered from these rivers over the years can hardly have been lost accidentally and it may well be that they represent votive offerings, perhaps to a river deity.

How can we best interpret the strong Central European (especially Hungarian) influences so evident on sites like Bor and Povegliano? R. Peroni and others have suggested that this is proof of an invasion of peoples from the Central Danube basin, people who put an end to Polada and introduced the rite of cremation to the Po Valley. This may be part of the story but, as we have seen, there is also plenty of evidence to suggest that many local traditions survived from earlier times, giving the Middle Bronze Age a distinctive North Italian character.

TERREMARE

A second densely populated area during the Middle and Late Bronze Age was centred on Emilia. The many settlements of this region were already well known before archaeologists came to take any interest in them, for their black organic soil, full of occupation debris, had long been used by the Emilian farmers as a fertilizer for their fields; this commercial exploitation unfortunately led to many of the sites being completely destroyed. The farmers called them *terremare* (black earth), a term which was adopted by the nineteenth-century prehistorians.

The Terremare settlements mostly lie along the margin of the plain following the line of the Apennine foot-hills in the provinces of Parma, Modena, and Bologna. Some are also found well out on the Plain as far as the Po and even beyond, in the provinces of Cremona and Brescia

Fig. 51   Section through rampart and ditch of a Terramara at Zaffanella, Mantua (after Parazzi)

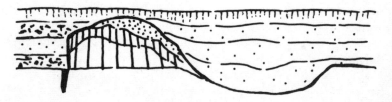

in Lombardy to the west and into the southern part of the Veneto in the east.

Many of these villages were extremely extensive and covered several acres, but their most distinguishing feature is the great depth of archaeological deposit which in some cases formed mounds standing up to twelve feet above the surrounding plain. This artificial elevation of the terremare was probably caused to a large extent by intentional dumping of rubbish in order to raise the settlement above flood danger level rather on a similar principle to the wooden *bonifiche* north of the Po.

An earthen bank and outer ditch enclosed many of the terremare. These banks were in some cases consolidated with rows of wooden posts or by means of well carpentered and continuous clay-filled wooden boxes, such as were preserved in the settlement of Castione dei Marchesi. Most prehistorians have interpreted these ramparts as a flood precaution, rather than as a strategic defence, although the double line of wooden stakes retaining the rampart of the settlement at Gottolengo (Brescia) could only have served for strategic defence, because this terramara is sited on a terrace well above the level of possible flooding.

Fig. 51

North of the Po, in the province of Verona, Zorzi excavated a remarkable defended settlement called the Castello del Tartaro which is probably the most north-easterly terramara. Set in the middle of marshy ground the earth rampart of the 'Castello' encloses an area of some 50 by 300 yards while in the interior an artificial *bonifica* platform of timbers had been laid to raise the whole level of the settlement. The site thus combines features of settlement construction of both the Veneto and Emilia.

Although large numbers of post holes were planned at Montale and other sites, no Terremare house plans are known. Circular mounds at Casa Cocconi (Reggio Emilia), rather similar to those in Early Bronze Age Lagazzi may, however, mark the position of huts or hearths.

Cattle and pig feature as the main livestock in the terremare and the bones of sheep, goat, horse and dog are also present. Wild game is common, comprising principally red deer, together with bear, wild boar, birds and fish. Vegetable remains also show a mixture of cultivated and wild fruits with wheat, lentils and beans on the one hand and hazel nuts, acorns, pears, apples, linseed, sloes, Cornel cherries and pistachio nuts on the other.

A great variety of finds from the terremare fill the showcases in the archaeological museums of Rome, Parma, Modena and Bologna. Pottery is especially abundant and in many respects resembles that of the Veneto. Greyish and black burnished pottery was used in the manufacture of the good-quality vessels. Carinated cups are a favourite form in this fabric, being usually embellished with an exuberantly decorated handle. These handles are mostly variations on the horned type and among them we find distinctively Terremaran inventions such as those with spectacle and handle-bar appendages. To the south-east of the Terremare area around Bologna crested, pillar and even bird terminal handles are more usual, suggesting links with Apennine and Venetian Bronze Age communities. Biconical jars, some with bosses on their bellies, are another familiar form here and in the Veneto, and both these and the cups often have rich grooved ornamentation. In coarse ware, simple cylindrical pots are usual, decorated only with applied cordons and pellets of clay. Cups with high swung cylindrical handles appear at a late stage of the Terremare culture as they do in the Apennine culture to the south.

Spindle whorls are common and suggest a lively textile industry, although few actual pieces of textile have survived. Bronze dress-fastening pins are present and we find again many of the same types that were popular in the Veneto. They include pins with spiral-wire heads, multiple ring heads and 'toggle' pins. The violin-bow fibula is a rare form but it is known on a few sites where the examples date to the final years of the Terremare settlements.

The inhabitants of the terremare continued to use 'v'-perforated buttons but more numerous finds are small perforated bone bars with dotted decoration, which were very probably also buttons.

These people seem to have taken more pride in personal appearance than many of their Bronze Age contemporaries in Europe, to judge from the number of razors and combs preserved on many sites. Their bronze razors were of distinctive double-edged type which were usually decorated with a central panel of cast openwork. Combs of both bronze and bone are found and in either material they were richly decorated.

The relative scarcity of weapons might well indicate a peaceful disposition, and indeed the few rather inefficient Terremare swords, with rounded rivetted heel plates, compare unfavourably with the

Plate 39

Fig. 47, c

Fig. 47, d

Fig. 53

Fig. 52

Fig. 50, a

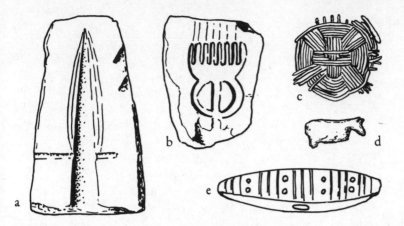

Fig. 52 a, b *Moulds for spear and comb from Casinalbo; c Basket from Castione; d Clay animal from Montale; e Bone toggle from Gorzano*

Fig. 53 a *Toggle pin; b Spiral wound-wire headed pin; c Triple ringheaded pin; d Tanged knife; e Medial flanged axe*

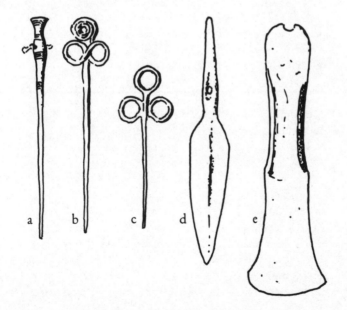

products of contemporary Central European swordsmiths. Bronze spears and arrows are also rare although a special type of bone arrow-head with a square or round sectioned head was produced in considerable quantities and in Emilia completely replaced the flint arrow-head. Wooden, club-headed arrows, for stunning birds and small game, were used and a fine example, decorated with incised triangles, came from Castione dei Marchesi.

Other metal tools are also comparable to those from the Veneto and include general-purpose knives or daggers with either rounded or trapezoidal rivetted heel plates during the earlier phases of Terremare, corresponding to Bor in the Veneto, and later types with flanged hilts or slender rivetted tangs like those found at Peschiera during the final

Fig. 50, d, e

Terremare development. Medial winged axes, bronze sickles and awls set in decorated bone handles are other usual metal implements.

A spade, a *baton* decorated with incised geometric designs, axe and sickle handles, and a composite wheel like one of the Mercurago wheels (see p. 74), feature among the wooden objects which were recovered in a good state of preservation from the waterlogged terramara of Castione.

Finally there is also the selection of bronze pendants, perforated teeth,

Plate 38,

Fig. 52, d

amber beads and also various bone discs, clay animal models, and model bone wheels which are recurrent features in most terremare.

The importance of the horse for traction is shown not only by the presence of horse bones on many sites but also by the occurrence of bone cheek-pieces from bits of a Central European type.

Bronze was worked within the bounds of the settlements, judging

Fig. 52, a, b

from the finds of stone casting moulds, slag and crucibles. The pro-duction of metalwork for local consumption within the many settlements probably accounts for the lack of hoards of metal objects that are a feature of Middle and Late Bronze Age communities elsewhere in Europe.

Several cremation cemeteries have been excavated in Emilia which must belong to the Terremare culture, though the poor quality of the cinerary urns and the absence of grave goods makes it difficult to date them accurately. Only at Montata (Reggio Emilia), in a burial area closely associated with a Terremare settlement were their characteristic pins and a violin-bow fibula preserved in the urns, while some of the urns themselves were covered with bowls which had Terremare-style horned handles. At Casinalbo, in a cemetery again not far away from a Terremare village, the burial urns were so densely packed that they had been stacked in two levels with some 40 urns per square yard. In other cemeteries such as Copezzato the funerary urns were more widely scattered over an area 100 yards in diameter.

The Terremare settlements in eastern Emilia, beyond Bologna and the River Reno, were in close contact with the Apennine Bronze Age people and a mixture of Terremare and Apennine Bronze Age pottery occurs on sites such as the large open settlement of Toscanella Imolese. In this area villages were often sited in positions with natural defences. Bertarina di Vecchiezzano (Forli), lying at the intersection of two rivers, and the continuing occupation on Monte Castellaccio in Imola are two such settlements.

Many myths have been woven around the terremare. During the nine-teenth century the archaeological world was confronted with the dogmatic theories of L. Pigorini who claimed that the Terremare people were the descendants of the Alpine lake dwellers who migrated south-wards to Emilia and here rebuilt their pile dwellings on dry land. He also maintained, on completely erroneous evidence, that the Terremare villages were built on a strict grid plan which was directly ancestral to the layout of a Roman camp, thus proving the Terremare people to be the forebears of the Romans.

However, it was also during the nineteenth century that the Terremare sites were first compared with Bronze Age settlement mounds of Hungary where sites such as Toszeg lie on the flat Danubian Plain, an environment remarkably comparable to the Po Valley. The connections in pottery and metalwork between Hungary and the Veneto, which we have already cited earlier, do indeed also apply in some degree, albeit less marked, to Emilia. The possibility, that an immigration of peoples from the central Danube at the start of the Middle Bronze Age led to the formation of the Terremare culture, cannot therefore be entirely ruled out.

THE MIDDLE AND LATE BRONZE AGE IN THE NORTH-WEST

From the beginning of the Middle Bronze Age onwards, north-western Lombardy, comprising the area from Milan northwards to the Lombard lakes, clearly emerges as a distinct cultural enclave, developing under the influence of Swiss and east French Bronze Age cultures.

Southern Lombardy, by contrast, was settled during this time by sporadic Terremare elements from across the Po, while to the east settlements in the Brescia region are related to the Middle Bronze Age of Garda.

Lake settlements continue to be occupied in northern Lombardy and perhaps new ones were even constructed. They are here mainly built on platforms consisting of dumped stones strengthened by wooden piles, a type of site which Swiss archaeologists of the nineteenth century called a *Steinberg*. The site of Bodio Centrale on Lake Varese was built in this way and comprised a circular area 40 yards in diameter. There were also two larger settlements on Lake Monate, at Pozzolo and Sabbione, which today lie under more than six feet of water. None of these sites have produced many bronze objects, but where they have been found these are Middle Bronze Age types such as 'toggle' pins, socketed spear-heads and medial winged axes. Bronze objects of this date have also been recorded from the former Polada settlements of Mercurago and Bosisio.

Bronze fish-hooks and large numbers of flint arrow-heads have been dredged up from these settlements, too, suggesting that, as in the Veneto, we are not dealing with purely agricultural communities.

There are few finds apart from these villages dating to the Middle Bronze Age in north-western Lombardy. An exception, however, is the important hoard of bronze objects from Cascina Ranza near Milan. The Cascina Ranza find consisted of two long solid-hilted daggers with curvaceous blades and incised decoration, the cast and decorated hilt of a sword of south German Spatzenhausen type, a rapier with a trapezoidal heel, 28 socketed lance-heads and 15 flanged axes with broad semi-circular cutting edges. This group of bronzes, while roughly of the same date as Bor and the early Terremare, is made up of objects whose cultural homeland is to be found in the Western Alps rather than in the Po Plain, or Hungary.

The cultural development of northern Lombardy becomes much clearer during the Late Bronze Age (the thirteenth century BC) with the appearance of a number of cremation cemeteries. To this period belong the cemetery of Scamozzina and the 18 burials from Monza. At Monza, burnt bones had been put in tall slender urns and sunk into pits surrounded by the remains of the funerary pyre and in some cases covered by stone slabs. Damaged grave goods were found in a few graves,

Fig. 54

consisting of razors with fret-decorated handles, 'toggle' and other kinds of pins. Of greater interest, however, are three swords, broken intentionally at the time of the burial, and put in with the burial urn. These have long, straight, parallel-sided blades with notched or tanged and rivetted hafts. Together with a number of other examples from Lombardy and Piedmont they belong to the so-called Rixheim-Monza school of sword production which flourished mainly on the Rhine and the Rhône on the other side of the Western Alps. The discovery of similar swords from the East Mediterranean provides us with valuable dating evidence, since an example found at Ugarit in Syria is conveniently inscribed with the cartouche of the Egyptian Pharoah Meremptah who reigned 1234–1220 BC.

Fig. 50, c, d

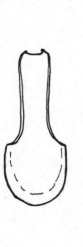

Fig. 54   Metalwork from the Cascina Ranza hoard

97

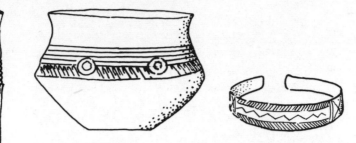

Fig. 55 Objects of the Canegrate culture. Pin and bowl from Canegrate, bracelet from Coarezzo. Pin and bowl 1 : 2

Fig. 55

Probably slightly later in date is the much larger urnfield excavated by Rittatore at Canegrate with more than 200 burials. The graves here were confined within a roughly elliptical area, at the two extremities of which were found traces of cremation pyres. The fine-ware urns from here were not at all like the Monza pottery, consisting for the most part of wide-mouthed, squat flask forms with concave necks and black-burnished surfaces. Decoration included grooved belly bosses and lines of parallel incisions. Coarser situlate vessels with splayed, slash-decorated rims and finger-nail impressions on the shoulder and body were also used.

The bronzes include a sword reminiscent of the Monza type, knives with openwork ring handles, and pins with expanded flat and biconical heads. Particularly distinctive of this cemetery were the bronze bracelets either with flat bands incised with geometric motifs or with spiral terminals which are comparable with the Geilspolsheim type of bracelet in the Western Alps.

A large hoard of bronzes from Ello (Como) also belongs to this horizon. In it were found a rivetted dagger, a flanged axe, a socketed spear-head, two notched and rivetted swords of the general Rixheim-Monza tradition, and a simple bronze cap helmet. This hoard could well be the full accoutrement of a Canegrate warrior.

Most of the parallels for Canegrate are with the West Alpine tradition of Reinecke's Bronze Age phase D, datable to the thirteenth century at the earliest.

The Canegrate culture, as Rittatore calls it, appears to stand in direct ancestral line to the Golasecca culture of the Iron Age, a role which has prompted Ritattore to give it the alternative name of the Proto-Golasecca culture (phase A).

CHAPTER VII

The Proto-Villanovans of the Final Bronze Age (1100–900 BC)

Shortly before 1100 BC a strikingly uniform culture is recognizable across the whole of Italy. Cremation cemeteries, which formerly had been restricted to the Po Valley, now appear all the way down the peninsula and even beyond the straits of Messina on the Milazzo promontory in Sicily. Traits in pottery and metalworking, which can be derived from the Central European Urnfield cultures, are closely connected with this new phenomenon, suggesting an influx of ideas or even people from across the Alps.

Fig. 56

What also strikes one immediately about the finds from these cemeteries is that they relate not to the earlier traditions of the Middle and Late Bronze Age but rather that they anticipate many of the types of artifacts produced by the Iron Age cultures which developed later in Central and Northern Italy. There seems to be little doubt that these people were the direct ancestors of many of the Iron Age peoples we will be discussing in the next chapters. The name Proto-Villanovan is thus perhaps as good as any for this group, since it carries with it the implication of the later destiny of the culture, namely its development into the Villanovan and other cultures of the Iron Age. An alternative term, Pianello-Timmari horizon, after two important cemeteries in Central and Southern Italy, can however also be used for this phase.

Several Proto-Villanovan settlements have also now been found in the North. Three of these lie well out in the middle of the eastern Po Plain: Mariconda on the banks of the River Po itself and Frattesine and Villamarzana further east near Rovigo. The Rocca di Rivoli in the foot-hills of the Alps was reoccupied by these people, and its strategic position on the Brenner route may well indicate a revived interest in transalpine traffic. The selection of a naturally fortified position for a settlement is again found at Vidolasco (Lombardy), a site recently excavated by V. Fusco.

A chain of villages and cemeteries can be traced along the axis of the River Po from Bissone (Pavia) in the west through Fontenella, Mariconda to Frattesine, suggesting the importance of this river as a line of communication during this period.

Frattesine must have been a village of considerable size, for surface finds on the site are strewn over an area of 700 by 190 yards. Excavations unearthed quantities of metalworking slag as well as lumps of blue and red glass, the raw material for manufacture of coloured beads. This must be the earliest evidence of glass-working in Italy, coincidentally near the modern glass-manufacturing town of Murano. Deer antler, sawn into lengths for the productions of a variety of tools, was also found in quantity.

Traces of similar industries were found at Mariconda, while not far from this settlement, at Merlara, one of the few hoards of Proto-Villanovan bronze objects from Northern Italy came to light in 1931. Winged axes, a lance-head, fragments of over 20 bronze sickles and ingots had been buried here in two bronze buckets. The large votive hoard from San Canziano just to the east of Trieste in the hills of Slovenia should also be mentioned here, since it contained an iron sword which is among the earliest objects of this metal to have been found in Europe. The position of this hoard no distance from the Postojna Pass underlines again the lively contact that now existed between Northern Italy and Central Europe.

The Merlara bronze vessels are typical of the new bronze products which appear now for the first time in Italy. The art of working sheet metal was probably introduced from the Danube basin and, in fact, one of the vessels from Merlara was a typical Central European bucket, of the so-called Kurd type, which remained popular in Italy well on into the Iron Age. Defensive armour, such as helmets and greaves, were also made from sheet bronze and the fine pair of metal greaves from Pergine (Trento), decorated with embossed designs which incorporate a decorative motif of the 'sun-boat and swan', long associated with the Central European Urnfield Culture, has been attributed to this phase on stylistic grounds by von Merhardt.

Plate 41

Solid-hilted bronze swords, imported from across the Alps, are known too from a few sites along the southern margin of the Alps as at Fumarago (Trento).

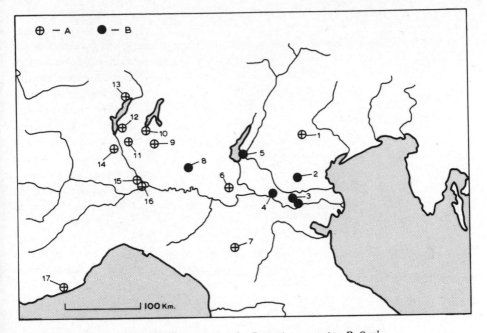

Fig. 56 Distribution of Proto-Villanovan sites. A Cremation cemeteries; B Settle-ments; 1 Angarano; 2 Este; 3 Frattesine; 4 Mariconda di Merlara; 5 Rivoli; 6 Fontanella; 7 Bismantova; 8 Vidolasco; 9 Biassone; 10 Como; 11 Canegrate; 12 Biadronno; 13 Ascona; 14 Galliate; 15 Bissone; 16 Badia; 17 Monte Grange

Vase-headed and globular or onion-headed dress pins with incised decoration copy Halstatt A models of the eleventh century BC north of the Alps, and improved fibulae come into use. These are larger than the Peschiera fibulae, having an arc-shaped bow, usually made from twisted wire, and were probably better suited for fastening heavy folds of cloth. Rectangular razors are also found.

Plate 40

Fig. 58

Proto-Villanovan cremation cemeteries have been found at Fontanella near Mantua in the Central Plain, and at Bismantova rather remotely situated in the upper reaches of an Apennine valley in Emilia, while smaller burial groups are known as far west as Bissone in southern Lombardy. The ashes were usually in biconical urns which often had a pronounced shoulder and a splayed rim. Bucket-shaped vessels were

Plate 40

sometimes used as well. The decoration of the urns frequently takes the form of vertical or oblique (turban) fluting on the shoulder or consists of bands of horizontal incisions below the rim and above the shoulder. Incised chevron bands combined with dots are another characteristic decorative device. Towards the end of this phase a technique of ornamenting pottery by impressions made with the twisted bow of a fibula or bracelet was introduced, known as the 'false-cord' method, a device which remained popular during the early part of the Iron Age.

Fig. 57   Many features of this ceramic tradition of shouldered urns, such as splayed rims, vertical and oblique fluting of the shoulder, or the bands of lines on the upper part of the urns, find striking parallels in the Hungarian Gava and Late Vattina pottery of the twelfth and thirteenth centuries, as well as in assemblages in eastern Austria, again evidence of strong cultural influences coming from the east.

The Proto-Villanovan culture did not prevail over the whole Plain and one is struck by the mutual exclusion of Proto-Villanovan and Terremare features. The Terremare culture may well have lingered on in Emilia although, in fact, there are no late finds from any Terremare sites to substantiate this idea. In nothern Lombardy the cemetery of Ascona on Lake Maggiore is roughly contemporary with Proto-Villanovan occupation to the east, to judge from the simple arc fibulae and 'false-cord' and turban decoration on the urns. However, the grave goods from this cemetery also include bracelets and pins of Canegrate type, which suggests that this area was not profoundly affected by events further east.

Fig. 57   Pottery from the Proto-Villanovan cemetery of Fontanella Mantovano (after Müller Karpe)

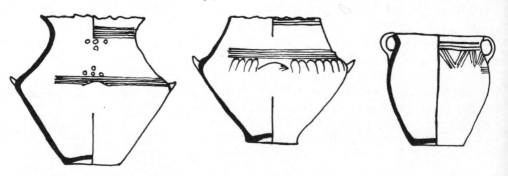

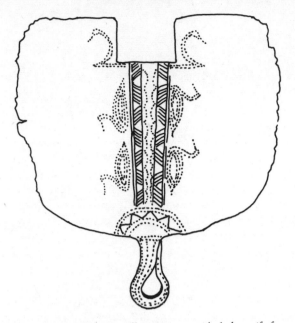

Fig. 58   Bronze razor of Proto-Villanovan type with duck motifs from the Proto-Villanovan cemetery of Bovolone (Verona) (after Fasani)

Rittatore in fact also calls Ascona Proto-Golasecca phase B to differentiate it from the Proto-Golaseccan A of Canegrate.

Many different hypotheses have been offered to explain the appearance of this Proto-Villanovan tradition in Italy. Säflund, von Merhardt and others considered that here was clear evidence of an invasion from Central Europe, but on the other hand Peroni and Bernabò Brea have more recently maintained that the Proto-Villanovan phenomenon represented nothing more than a local development from the Apennine Bronze Age culture, and Trump suggests that it may have developed from the Terremare.

Looking at the finds from the Po Plain one is, however, impressed first by the break with earlier cultures and secondly by the parallels in pottery and metal objects, found across the Eastern Alps. If there was not an actual invasion from the east at this time, the lands on either side of the Alps may well have been brought together under some sort of centralized political control, very similar to the situation we have seen twice before, during the Early and Middle to Late Bronze Ages.

CHAPTER VIII

The Early Iron Age

The firm line that students of Italian prehistory usually draw at 900 B C, between the outgoing Bronze Age and the start of the Age of Iron, is in many respects misleading, for it does not in fact mark any real break in the life of the prehistoric populations envolved. If the archaeological record is interpreted aright, the transition between the Late and the Final Bronze Age, when new ideas and perhaps peoples infiltrated from the north-east, was a far more traumatic episode.

The new material, iron, which was now coming into use for the first time had little economic impact on the life of the inhabitants of Northern Italy during the initial phases of the Iron Age. Bronze was still the main metal for their everyday tools and ornaments and it was not until the Celts arrived in the late fifth century that Iron to any extent replaced the widespread use of bronze.

There was, however, one significant fact about the populations of the ninth century B C, which can only be appreciated with hindsight, and that was that the settlements and cemeteries which came into existence at this time were soon to become the centres of large permanent population concentrations of the Iron Age civilizations. During the first half of the first millennium, some of these centres developed into the first real towns in the north, as was the case at Bologna and probably also at Este and Padua, while everywhere we can see a rapid increase in population and

Fig. 59 the onset of a long period of stable prosperity.

During the Middle and Late Bronze Age three separate cultural areas had developed in the Veneto, Emilia and north-western Lombardy. Although partly obscured by the Proto-Villanovan episode, it is interesting to see that at about 900 B C these same three areas re-emerged to take on even more individual cultural characteristics. For we find now the Iron Age cultures of Bologna in Emilia, Golasecca in Lombardy and Este in the Veneto starting their long and steady separate evolution, which was only terminated by the irruption of the Celtic tribes onto the Po Plain in about the fifth century and, in the case of Este, by the Romans several centuries later.

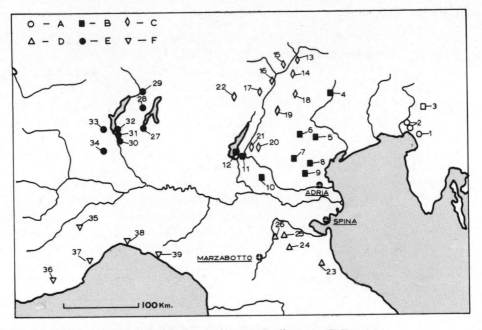

*Fig. 59   Iron Age settlements in Northern Italy; A Castellieri sites; B Este sites;
C Melaun—San Zeno sites; D Emilian Villanovan sites; E Golasecca sites;
F Ligurian sites; 1 Monte S. Leonardo; 2 Redipuglia and Doberdo; 3 Santa Lucia
(Idria); 4 Lagole; 5 Montebelluna; 6 Angarona; 7 Vicenza; 8 Padua; 9 Este;
10 Oppeano; 11 Forte di Rivoli; 12 Garda; 13 Melaun-Meluno; 14 Schlern—
Sciliar; 15 Collalbo-Klobstein; 16 Pfatten—Vadena; 17 San Zeno; 18 Bellamonte;
19 Montesei; 20 Monte Loffa; 21 Sottosengia; 22 Dos dell'Arca; 23 Forli;
24 Imola; 25 Villanova; 26 Bologna; 27 Ca' Morta; 28 Caslé di Ramponio;
29 Bellinzona; 30 Sesto Calende; 31 Golasecca; 32 Castelletto Ticino; 33 Ameno;
34 S. Bernardino di Briona; 35 Bec Berciassa; 36 Monte Bignone; 37 Arene
Candide; 38 Genoa; 39 Chiavari*

It is interesting to note that these Iron Age cultures, like their Bronze
Age precursors, continued to be influenced from across the Alps by the
final stages of the Central European Urnfield culture, as well as by the
Hallstatt Iron Age culture of the seventh and sixth centuries B C.

Before describing the individual Iron Age groups, it would be as well
to look at the north in its wider context of the whole Italian Iron Age.
Some of the main problems have been discussed already in other books
in this series, notably Hugh Hencken's *Tarquinia and Etruscan Origins*

and David Trump's *Central and Southern Italy*. We have seen how on purely archaeological evidence the Proto-Villanovan urnfields could be taken to represent an intrusion of peoples from Central Europe and it will later be evident that the cultures of the Iron Age are largely rooted in Proto-Villanovan tradition. The Villanovan culture of Tuscany which gave birth to the Etruscan civilization of the eighth century BC likewise had a Proto-Villanovan background. It is here however that we run up against a major contradiction from the linguistic evidence, for the later bearers of the Este culture, the Veneti, spoke an Indo-European language, whereas the Etruscans, as is well known, did not. We are thus brought face to face with the sobering reality that linguistic groupings do not necessarily coincide with the distribution of archaeological cultures. As we shall see later, the same difficulty of correlation arises in the case of the La Tène culture and the Celtic language.

The question, where the Early Italian Iron Age is concerned, as to whether the material culture or the linguistic grouping is the more significant, is a crucial one, for changes can occur in one with little corresponding change in the other. Both bodies of evidence have their own validity in the reconstruction of ancient society and both should be respected. If the Etruscan language was indigenous, and not an introduction from the Eastern Mediterranean during the eighth century, the Indo-European language of the Veneto could also be seen as having an ancestry going back to the Early Bronze Age at least.

BOLOGNA AND THE VILLANOVAN CULTURE (900–525 BC)

The main urban centre of the North Italian Plain during the Iron Age was Bologna, a town which grew and prospered on the River Reno at the eastern end of the principal route across the Apennines to Tuscany.

The first important discoveries relating to the Iron Age of Bologna, made in 1853, were not from the city itself, but at Villanova, a hamlet some four miles distant from Bologna, on the estate of Count Gozzadini, the man who was subsequently responsible for excavating many of the major Iron Age cemeteries in Bologna itself.

The name of Villanova has, during the last hundred years, gathered considerable notoriety, being used to describe the whole pre-Etruscan Iron Age development not only of Emilia and the Po Plain, but of Tuscany as well.

The first Villanovans were probably, in part, descended from local Proto-Villanovan communities and the Proto-Villanovan cemetery of Bismantova (Reggio Emilia) already contained metal types such as the lunate razor, which is Iron Age rather than Final Bronze Age in date.

At the same time we can see, among the finds from the first Iron Age cemeteries, features which are closely paralleled across the Apennines and which have been interpreted as a penetration of peoples from Tuscany. These similarities however are perhaps better seen as a parallel development of two communities in close contact on either end of a trade route. These 'Tuscan' features include fibulae with disc or spiral catch-plates and narrow two-storied cinerary urns, which are both usual Tuscan types; indeed, the growth of a town at Bologna itself is comparable to the emergence of the first towns at Veii, Tarquinia and other centres of Villanovan Etruria.

Fig. 61, c
Fig. 60, a

A third ingredient in the make-up of the early stages of the Bologna Iron Age is the continuing tradition of Central European Urnfield features which permeated the early years of all the Italian Iron Age cultures from Tuscany to the Alps. It makes itself apparent especially in the metalwork where, for example, we find beaten bronze vessels and belt plates, embellished with embossed dotted designs which often include the Urnfield device of the 'sunboat and swan'.

The Villanovan stage lasted at Bologna until about 525 BC when, with the appearance of the later Etruscans in Emilia, a strong element of classical culture was introduced.

During this period Bologna remained the focal point of trade and culture in Emilia. There were indeed other settlements, as at Imola and Forli, but these were mere villages compared with the great urban centre on the River Reno. The disposition of the cemeteries encompassing ancient Bologna to the east, west and south, together with the great concentration of occupation debris found in many parts of the city, show that from its inception or at least from the eighth century, it was a settlement of more than a mile in diameter. Although G. Mansuelli and others have claimed that Bologna was at first a collection of villages, rather than a town, there is no reason to doubt some over-all urban organization for this community.

Within the city, the Iron Age finds have often been associated with regular circular pits, which have rightly or wrongly been interpreted as hut floors. Their similarity to the Neolithic pits which we have already discussed is quite striking and it is possible that they were, in fact, used for some sort of storage rather than for habitation. These settlement remains unfortunately tell us little about the internal layout of the town or about its economic life. What we know about Iron Age Bologna and its development comes, in fact, almost entirely from the large cremation cemeteries on the perimeter of the settlement.

To the east, towards Imola, lay the early cemeteries of San Vitale and Savena, with together more than a thousand graves, while westwards, lining the old road up the Reno valley and the Apennine pass, cemeteries with many thousands of burials have been excavated in the Fondo Benacci and Fondo Arnoaldi.

Cremation in urns remained throughout the predominant rite, although during the seventh or sixth century (the Arnoaldi phase) inhumation and cremation in large jars (*dolia*) were also introduced, presumably from Tuscany, where both are known at an earlier date.

Although the graves of the ninth century are provided with only a few basic necessities, a razor, fibulae, bracelets and pins, by the eighth some graves have a more extensive range of metal vessels and equipment which reflect increasing prosperity and even, perhaps, the rise of a merchant class. An exceptional burial like grave no. 39 from the Benacci-Caprara cemetery contained a varied assortment of metal vessels, pottery, bronze axes, a knife, a razor, fibulae and pins, as well as a bronze sword and a *Fig. 60, e-g* bridle bit. The social status of such an individual is difficult to judge, but the grave does not really have the distinguishing features of a prince's grave and could well be that of a wealthy trader or industrialist.

From the eighth century onwards Bologna became the major centre of bronze technology on the Po Plain, the 'Birmingham of North Italy' as Randall MacIver once described it. This industrial prominence can in part be explained by the fact that much of the copper used was imported directly down the Reno valley from Tuscany. Later, during the sixth century, when iron started to become more important, this metal too would have been carried eastwards by the same route. Evidence of a developed bronze technology is to be seen in the great variety of objects of cast and beaten bronze from the graves, as well as in the great hoard of bronzes from San Francesco, which shows us something of the scale of metalworking at this time. This find, contained in a great pottery storage jar, was made up of no less than 14,838 objects, which had apparently been collected for scrap, and is one of the largest hoards ever to be found in Europe.

During its four hundred years of existence the Villanovan culture of Bologna naturally went through several stages of development, but the repeated attempts by prehistorians to describe and define this cultural evolution has led to confusion rather than clarification of what actually took place.

Fig. 60 Bologna Iron Age. a, b Bologna I urn and bracelet from the San Vitale cemetery; c Bologna II razor from San Vitale; d Axe from the San Francesco hoard; e–g Bronze vessels from the rich grave no. 39 at Benacci-Caprara; h, i Arnoaldi urn and dipper (after Müller Karpe)

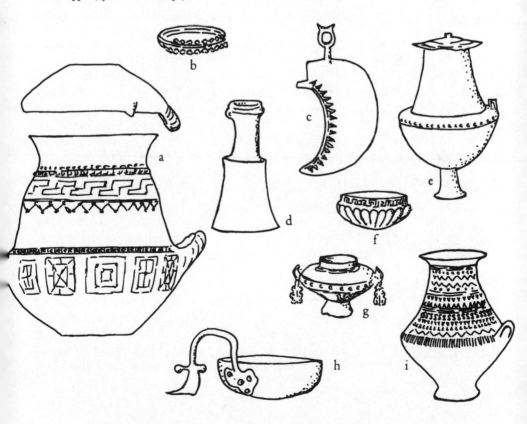

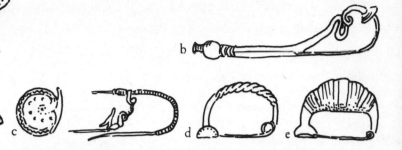

A well-worn triple division of the Bologna sequence, first worked out by Brizio, Montelius and Grenier at the end of the nineteenth century, is still widely employed with the main cemeteries giving their names to the individual phases. These are Benacci I (900–750 BC), Benacci II (750–630 BC) and Arnoaldi (630–525 BC). Following the publication of the cemetery of San Vitale in 1913, an archaic phase of Benacci I, called appropriately the San Vitale phase, was also added to the sequence. The terms Villanovan I to IV can be used as an alternative nomenclature.

Recently, Professor H. Müller Karpe has shown that former definitions of the San Vitale and Benacci stages are unsatisfactory, and with a masterful re-examination of the San Vitale and Savena cemeteries he has abandoned the old terminology for these early stages and introduced new phases which cut right across the former classification. These are Bologna I, 900–800 BC (comprising San Vitale and part of Benacci I), Bologna II, 800–700 BC (the rest of Benacci I and part of Benacci II), and Bologna III which overlaps the end of Benacci II and the start of Arnoaldi. Unfortunately at present Müller Karpe's scheme can be applied only to the metal objects from the tombs and only Bologna I and II have been adequately defined, so that one still has to use both terminologies. Müller Karpe's Bologna I and II are used here for the early stages and the old term Arnoaldi (Villanovan IV) for the later development.

The two phases Bologna I and II both show considerable similarity with the first and second periods of the southern Villanovan culture of Tuscany. From 700 onwards, however, development in the two areas appears to get out of step, the Orientalizing influences from the east rapidly transforming the south into the Etruscan civilization, which

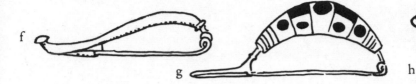

Fig. 61 a Bronze antennae hilted sword from Castione della Presolana, 1 : 3;
b Arnoaldi serpentine fibula; c Disc-footed fibula from San Vitale (Bologna I);
d Arc fibula with thickened twisted bow from San Vitale (Bologna I); e Leech fibula
(Bologna II); f Certosa fibula; g Arnoaldi fibula with bone and amber decorated bow;
h Iron sword with bronze pommel from below the Forte di Rivoli, 1 : 4

finds only faint echoes in the contemporary culture of Arnoaldi in
Bologna.

The metalwork of Bologna I, as we have already said, shows little
variety. Men were buried with razors, as they were during the Proto-
Villanovan period but instead of being of the double-edged variety these
now had a single cutting edge shaped like a half moon. Their womenfolk usually wore bronze wire bracelets with distinctive undulating
terminals. Many of the fibulae are directly evolved from the simple
Proto-Villanovan arc type, differing only in now having a thicker cast
bow, but the complicated two-part brooch with a serpentine bow and
large spiral hammered catch-plate was also in fashion and is one of the
southern Villanovan types which are rare elsewhere in the Po Valley.

The bronzes of Bologna II are characterized by a slightly broader
lunate razor and a fibula with an even thicker bulbous bow, the so-
called 'leech' type. The bows of these leech fibulae are sometimes made
up by threading discs of bone or amber on to a central wire support. A
much richer assortment of metal goods also characterizes this period.
Swords with antennae hilts, the most popular sword type during the
Iron Age in Northern Italy, and swords with simpler rounded pommels,
are now found. Swords, however, are not common in graves nor were
there many (only 19) among the many thousands of other items in the
great San Francesco hoard; perhaps this is an indication of the unwarlike
character of society in Bologna at this time.

This same San Francesco hoard, which although probably deposited
early in the seventh century has mainly Bologna II material, gives us a
good cross-section of bronze objects in use during the eighth century.
There were, for example, 3,952 axes mostly of a socketed type with a

Fig. 62 Stamped pottery decoration of the North Italian Iron Age. a *Arnoaldi pottery from Bologna;* b *Golasecca III A pottery;* c *Ligurian pottery from Chiavari;* d *San Zeno pottery from the province of Trento.*

spade-shaped blade, 21 daggers, 79 knives, 24 saws, 398 chisels and gouges, 412 sickles, as well as 77 razors, 3,206 fibulae, 107 belt plates and 70 horse-bits.

Bronze horse-bits are particularly common in Bologna from Bologna II times onwards, and they are commonly found in pairs in graves. Their cheek-pieces are often finely cast in openwork designs which are either geometric or sometimes themselves in the form of horses. Bits like these are also found in contemporary graves of the southern Villanovans.

In Bologna II the craft of making sheet-metal vessels was brought to a fine art, and a diversity of forms was produced. Fluted basins, handled vases, situlate buckets of the Kurd type, ladles, and even metal copies of clay cinerary urns were manufactured. A particularly fine collection of

Fig. 60, e–g

bronze vessels was found in the rich grave 39 in the Benacci-Caprara cemetery.

Fig. 61, b, g

The metalwork of the periods following Bologna II after 700 B C shows a steady but uninspired development. The leech and serpentine fibulae are produced now with increasingly lengthened catch-plates. The dragon type of fibula is fashionable during the sixth century. Sheet-metal production continues to thrive and we find, during Arnoaldi, a cylindrical bucket with horizontal cordons being produced which is very distinctive of this period. Iron now increasingly replaces bronze as a material for everyday equipment.

An evolution in pottery style can also be recognized throughout the development of the Villanovan culture. The early cinerary urns of Bologna I and II show close similarities with contemporary pottery on the other side of the Apennines, with their slender biconical outline, offset rounded shoulder, everted rim and single horizontal handles. The rich multilinear incised key patterns and other geometric designs which decorate them is also paralleled in Tuscany. The style of these urns apparently changed little during the eighth century.

The urns were often covered by inverted bowls of a type with a single handle and incurving rim which were decorated in a similar manner to the urns. Accessory vessels include small handled cups, pedestalled bowls, double cups and pottery copies of the metal Kurd situlae.

b

Some of the bowls and double cups have horses modelled into their handles. A unique vessel found in a grave, at Benacci, probably of Bologna II date, is a little askos in the form of a horned animal surmounted by a horse and rider, and decorated with 'false cord' impressions.

During the Arnoaldi period the potters' wheel was introduced and a rather elegant series of biconical urns and pottery situlae were produced. A novel method of impressed decoration was also developed using a variety of specially prepared stamps bearing designs of circles, triangles, crosses, rosettes and even ducks and human figures.

The Arnoaldi stage of Bologna's Villanovan development reflects little of the glamour of contemporary southern Etruria with its rich circle and tumulus burials and oriental style metalwork. Only in the Arsenale grave at Bologna was there found a gold fibula decorated with fine granular designs, which was probably manufactured across the Apennines in Vetulonia.

c

Plate 42

Plates 44, 45

Fig. 62, a

THE CERTOSA PHASE AT BOLOGNA AND THE ETRUSCANS IN THE PO VALLEY

We have seen in the last section that although strong contacts existed between Bologna and Tuscany during the early part of the Iron Age these diminished after 700 B C. Elsewhere in the North evidence of direct contacts with Tuscany are everywhere meagre before the fifth century. Exceptions include the fine crested Villanovan helmet of eighth-century date, dredged from the River Tanaro at Alessandria (Piedmont), which must have come from Tuscany, and the ornate figured bronze vessel from the Golasecca cemetery of Castelletto Ticino, at the southern end of Lake Maggiore, probably made in Etruria during the Orientalizing period of the seventh century.

Towards the end of the sixth century B C the Etruscans appear to have established some kind of political control over at least part of the Po Plain, which lasted well into the fifth century. According to Etruscan historians, a federation of twelve towns was created which probably included Marzabotto (Misa), Bologna (Felsina), Mantua, Parma, Modena, Piacenza, Rimini, Ravenna, Melzo – a site which is possibly to be identified with Melzo near Milan – and the ports of Spina and Adria.

d

Archaeological traces of this Etruscan domination, as distinct from trade, are however scarce, the most concrete evidence coming from Bologna and central Emilia, the areas closest to Etruria.

Evidence for this period at Bologna, or *Felsina* as it was known to the Etruscans, is mainly from a cemetery at Certosa, which lies on the road to the north-west out of Bologna, beyond the Benacci and Arnoaldi cemeteries.

During this Certosa phase (525–400) commerce was developed and the city prospered. Luxury Greek Attic black-figure and red-figure pottery, imported through the Adriatic ports of Adria and Spina, now put an end to the local tradition of fine ceramics, while household wares take on an increasingly classical character. Likewise, bronze flagons and wine pots made in the factories of Vulci and other towns in Etruria competed with the local bronze industry. The manufacture of sheet-bronze vessels still flourished, however, and a popular utility product was the bronze cylindrical bucket similar to those made during the Arnoaldi phase, but now with close set, instead of widely spaced, horizontal cordons.

The *pièce de resistance* of the metalwork from the Certosa cemetery is a bronze situla, beautifully decorated with embossed figures arranged in zones, belonging to the tradition of decorated situlae and other sheet-metal work which was being developed at about this time in the Veneto and the Eastern Alps (described in more detail on p. 121). Although it may be an import from the north, stylistic considerations suggest that it was probably manufactured in Emilia, perhaps by emigré artisans. Other examples of this Emilian situla art comprise, for instance, the shield-boss ornamented with two embossed warriors found at Carpena, and two bronze mirrors, with finely engraved backs, from Arnoaldi and Galassina di Castelvetro (Modena), which caricature the elegant classical-style mirrors of Etruria.

The evolution of the fibula is taken a stage further during this period. The elaborations found in earlier fibulae are done away with and a simple brooch with a terminal button on the catch-plate, the Certosa fibula, is the most distinctive type in fashion.

Fig. 61, f

The burial rite in the Certosa cemetery included both inhumation and cremation, and some of the graves were marked with carved lime-stone gravestones, a practice which in fact was first introduced during the

Arnoaldi period. At first these grave markers are shaped rather like the
stylized head and shoulders of a human figure, but the later examples Plate 43
are just elongated oval slabs. The carving on these stones is in a clean
bas-relief style, and both the design of the slabs and the decoration show
little connection with contemporary Etruria. During the sixth century
Orientalizing designs, perhaps inspired directly from the eastern
Mediterranean, are usual and feature sphinxes or the 'tree of life' flanked
by rampant heraldic beasts. Later however, in the full Certosa period,
they more often carry scenes representing warriors in combat, on foot or
on horseback, which may record for posterity the warlike exploits of the
dead. At the same time inscriptions in Etruscan appear on the margins
of some of these stones.

Whereas the indigenous inhabitants of Bologna seem to have acquired
no more than a veneer of Etruscan culture, there is one site about which
there is little doubt as to its pure Etruscan character. This is Marzabotto,
the ancient town of Misa, on the route up the River Reno to the Apennine
passes. Excavations which are still being continued by Mansuelli, have
laid bare a large part of an Etruscan town, whose remains have fortunately
not been disfigured by later occupation. Covering an area nearly two
miles across, Misa was a new town laid out by the Etruscans on the classical grid plan of streets and rectangular house blocks, and must have been
the first regularly planned settlement of its kind north of the Apennines.
A temple area on a low acropolis dominated the main town and a
cemetery of well-constructed stone tombs was found nearby. As a
settlement established and developed perhaps in connection with the
Etruscan expansion into the Po Plain, Misa was completely abandoned
after its capture, and its short occupation, by the Celts in the fourth
century BC.

The archaeological evidence for deeper Etruscan penetration of the
Plain, claimed by Etruscan legend, is less satisfactory. Other sites in
Emilia producing evidence of Etruscan occupation include a settlement
at Servirola San Polo (Reggio Emilia) on the River Enza, and what
may be a temple at Persolino (Faenza). An inhumation burial from
Fraore (Parma), accompanied by gold Certosa fibulae, serpentine Plate 46
fibulae and a pair of intricate gold filigree ear-rings of Etruscan manufacture, could either be the grave of an Etruscan or a rich native. Traded
goods apart, traces of an Etruscan presence north of the Po are limited to

Plate 47

finds from Rivalta (Mantua); some enigmatic inhumation burials found at Remedello (Brescia), which were associated with a large quantity of pottery, including Etruscan *bucchero* cups, remarkable fluted pedestalled vessels and two statuettes of skirted figures; and clear signs of Etruscan activity in the ports of Spina and Adria.

THE VENETI AND THE ESTE CULTURE

During the ninth century B C there emerged in the north-eastern area of the Po Plain, between the Rivers Mincio and Livenza, a dynamic and independent Iron Age culture, which survived some seven centuries before finally being submerged by the expanding rule of Rome. The archaeological remains of these Iron peoples are called by prehistorians the Este or Atestine culture, after their principal settlement Ateste (today Este) south of the Euganean Hills. To the Greeks and Romans, however, these people were known as the Veneti (Enevtoi), a name which is still used today to describe the territory in which they once lived.

Finds of the Este culture come from a rather small number of population centres, some of which must have been fair-sized towns by the time the Romans arrived. Este, Padua, Vicenza and Oppeano (Verona) were probably the largest and main settlement sites on the Plain. The Este culture also penetrated the mountain valleys of the Rivers Piave and Brenta in the north-east and outposts were established to the west as far as Lake Garda. The naturally defended position on the Forte di Rivoli, about a mile north of the Neolithic and Bronze Age settlement on the Rocca di Rivoli, may have been established about 800 B C to secure the border between the Este group of peoples and the ancestors of the Raeti, who lived further up the Adige valley in the foot-hills of the Alps. Hill settlements are also known in the Berici and Euganean Hills, for example Monte Lozzo, close to the main Este towns.

The port of Adria, in the southern part of the Venetian territory, flourished from the sixth century onwards, providing the people of Este with a trade outlet to the Adriatic.

At Este and Padua, the largest towns, little of the ancient settlement has survived the continuous occupation of the sites since prehistoric times. Both towns, like Iron Age Bologna, were apparently undefended, although it can be noted that Padua was strategically sited at the confluence of two rivers.

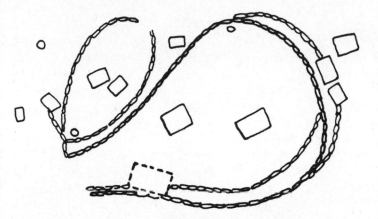

Fig. 63   Este. Burials and stone walled cemetery enclosure of the Este III period

At Padua, wooden structures found buried beneath some eighteen feet of silt have been interpreted as the remains of a building protected by a dam of tree trunks, while elsewhere in the city circular huts have been brought to light. Remains of wooden *bonifica* type platforms for consolidating the subsoil have also been found at Este, and here the houses so far unearthed have been rectangular with daub walls, clay floors and built-in, raised, rectangular clay hearths. Solid clay fire-dogs sometimes decorated with incised geometric patterns or else ornamented with rams' heads were used for supporting cooking grills over the hearths during the early phases of Este, although by the fifth century these had been supplanted by dogs of bronze and iron.

Fig. 64, c

It is to the cemeteries that we again have to turn for most of our knowledge of the Este culture. Burial rite was cremation in an urn, which at Este was usually placed in a stone cist. During the late sixth century, however, urns and grave goods were sometimes buried in large jars, a custom perhaps borrowed from contemporary Bologna.

The external structure of the graves shows a certain amount of regional variation and, for example at Este, the cemeteries were often divided up into rectangular family burial plots by vertical slab walls and the whole cemetery itself was surrounded by a similar wall.

Fig. 63

Surface markers on individual graves in the form of stones or a rough cairn appear in the second phase of Este, and dressed stone pillars with inscriptions in the local Venetic script come in in the fifth century (Este

III). At Padua in the fourth and third centuries graves were sometimes marked by rectangular grave stones finely carved with figured scenes in low relief. At Mel (Belluno) the cemetery layout was again different with important graves marked by stone circles between 6 and 9 feet in diameter, reminiscent of the circle graves of Etruscan Vetulonia, interspersed among more numerous cist graves.

The standard grave goods usually comprise a pottery urn and a metal fibula. Many burials, however, have more than this bare minimum and large numbers of accessory vessels are common from the second period of Este onwards. As at Bologna there is no clear distinction between rich and poor recognizable among the grave goods, nor any evidence of a wealthy upper stratum of society such as we find in the Celtic world or even in the Golasecca culture of Lombardy and in Etruria. An important burial dating to the second half of the eighth century (Este II), grave no. 236 in the Ricovero cemetery at Este, in fact gives us a further idea of what Este society was like at the time. As H. Frey has pointed out, the man buried here seems to have been both a warrior and a craftsman, for he had with him an antennae sword, a lunate razor, a saw, a chisel, a knife, axes and a bronze situla. Here are none of the rich trappings of a chieftain but, as in the case of the Benacci-Caprara grave at Bologna, this seems to have been a man who acquired his wealth perhaps through trade and handiwork.

At the end of the nineteenth century A. Prosdocimi, the director of the Este Museum, was able to propose a fourfold chronological division of the Este culture, between the ninth and the second century BC, based on a study of the associated finds from the many thousands of graves which he had excavated in the neighbourhood of the town. Although Prosdocimi's four phases remain basically unchanged, G. Fogolari and H. Frey have recently subdivided the long second and third phases so that we now have a far more detailed picture of the evolution of this culture than was previously available.

The sequence starts with Este I (900–750) when the number of graves at Este itself indicates that there was only a small nucleus of population living on the site. We have on the other hand much more information about this first phase from two cemeteries on the very fringe of Este's territory, one at Angarano (Bassano) and the other at Garda, on the lake of the same name. The 119 burials from Angarano show that this cemetery is one of the few sites which spans the transition from the Proto-Villanovan to the first stage of the Iron Age, leaving us in no doubt as to the immediate origins of the Este culture.

In Este II (750–575), now subdivided into three phases by Fogolari and Frey, a rapid growth in the population and wealth of the village at Este is evident and trade contacts both with Central Italy and the Orient are established by the end of this phase.

During Este III (575–350) the Iron Age reaches its most prosperous development, while in Este IV (350–182), also now subdivided into three sub-phases, the culture becomes increasingly infiltrated with foreign ideas, first from the Celtic world and finally from Rome.

The material culture evolves gradually throughout the sequence and in several respects this follows the cultural evolution of urban Bologna to the south across the Po.

The Este people were competent potters and the development of their pottery styles shows ingenuity as well as an aesthetic appreciation of ceramic design. The urns of Este I differed little from the local Proto-Villanovan urns found at Fontanella and Mariconda for they have the same wide biconical outline with a pronounced shoulder and splayed rim as well as similar grooved and 'false-cord' decoration. Situlate pots are another inherited form.

Fig. 64 Objects from Este III graves. a Amber beads; b Coral beads; c Bronze fire dog; d 'Kurd' situla (after Frey and Fogolari)

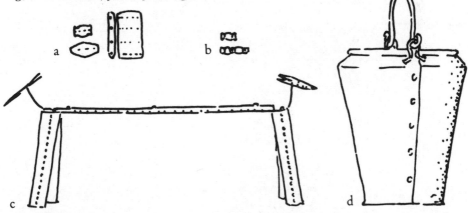

Plate 50

One remarkable and unique vessel, in the form of two birds perched one on top of the other, decorated with 'false-cord' and mounted on wheels, was found in a rich grave in the Pelà cemetery at Este. It reminds one immediately of the combined horse, rider and horned beast, decorated in an identical manner, from the Benacci cemetery in Bologna, and it is also clearly related to the whole series of bird vessels found, from Etruria to Central Europe, during the first half of the first millennium B C. Although bird vessels of this type are usually regarded as connected with the bird symbolism which permeates most of the cultures that had anything to do with the Late Bronze Age Urnfield tradition of Central Europe, the fact that a similar bird vessel was found at Veii in Etruria in a child's grave has led J. Close-Brooks to the conclusion that these objects were toys. It is probably significant therefore that one of the vessels from the Pelà grave appears to be a feeding bottle.

The pottery of Este II is a stage further removed from its Proto-Villanovan ancestry, although the biconical urn, somewhat taller and more flamboyant, and the situla, now more like its bronze prototypes, are still standard cremation containers and 'false cord' decoration continues to be used. New are the low bowls with in-turned rims, cups on tall pedestals, and cups with high loop handles. Incisions are used to make lively geometric decoration and designs even include stylized horses.

Plate 51

Plate 53

A new technique of pottery decoration, introduced from Central Europe, was the practice of impressing bronze studs into the surface of the pottery so as to make simple geometric patterns (meanders, running spirals, etc.) and perhaps also to make the pots look like more expensive embossed metal vessels. More unusual products of the Este II pottery include a delightful little vessel in the shape of a pig and another in the form of a boot.

Plate 52

In Este III the pottery is wheel-turned and becomes much more professional in design. Most of the fine pottery is now decorated with horizontal zones of red and black paint, separated by narrow cordons. The range of these vessels includes a situlate pot with a neatly fitting lid which is now the usual container for cremations. Equally distinctive are the tall pedestalled bowls decorated in the same way. The technique of impressed stamp decoration is found on some vessels but it is not as popular as it was in Bologna.

Finally, in Este IV, the pottery degenerates and mass-produced, poorly decorated vessels copying both Greek and Celtic originals are manufactured.

In Este the changing fashions in fibulae closely follow the trends in design already seen in Bologna. Evolving from the simple arc fibula of Proto-Villanovan times we find, in turn, the type with a slightly thickened bow in Este I, leech and serpentine fibulae in Este II, with the tendency for long catch-plates at the end of this period, and the Certosa and dragon fibulae in Este III. During Este IV, Celtic La Tène brooches become fashionable and these are eventually replaced by Roman types. Again like the inhabitants of Bologna, the Este people were accomplished in the art of sheet-bronze working. In fact during the sixth and fifth centuries they excelled the bronze-smiths of Bologna in the production of finely decorated metalwork, for it was here that one of the principal centres of the fine 'situla art' bronze products was located.

The main vehicle for this art style was the shouldered bronze situla which was a direct descendant of the Kurd type of bucket, first seen in the Po Plain during Proto-Villanovan times (Merlara) and which remained a familiar household object throughout the early development of Este. During the seventh century in Austria (Klein Glein) and in Lombardy (Sesto Calende) some of these situlae were already decorated with zones of simple repoussée dot-outlined figures of men and animals. In the sixth century, however, Orientalizing motifs copied from Etruscan metalwork and Corinthian pottery appear in combination with a new technique of figure embossing also of eastern inspiration, which become the basic ingredients of the situla art.

Fig. 64, d

This art style is not only restricted to situlae – although these offered the maximum scope for the development of design – but at Este was also applied to lids for these vessels, to sheet-bronze dagger sheaths, helmets, belt plates and votive plaques, while in Emilia shield bosses and mirrors were decorated in the same style. Whereas the designs on the situlae were always embossed, some of the other objects, helmets, sheaths, belt plates and mirrors, had the designs engraved on them.

Fig. 65

Although the greatest variety of objects decorated in the situla style are to be found in the Este culture, and although Este was probably the main centre of this artistic tradition, it was only one workshop in a chain of production centres which extended across the Eastern Alps (Austria

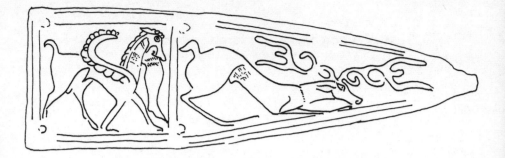

and Slovenia) through the Veneto to Emilia and the Alpine provinces of Trento and Bolzano.

One of the earliest situlae decorated in this style is the example from the Benvenuti grave at Este, which was accompanied by grave goods dating to the transition between Este II and III (*c.* 575 BC). Although rather primitive in character, still making extensive use of the old technique of repoussée dotted lines, it displays most of the basic features of the situla art style. In the three registers we find the little human figures with their caricature faces, big noses and puffed out cheeks, which are used through-out the situla art. In the top band are scenes of daily life interspersed with plants, a bird and a centaur; below this a frieze of deer, griffens and sphinxes, and at the bottom are warriors, chariots and a battle scene.

More elaborate and better executed scenes in the same vein are found on the situlae of the later sixth and fifth centuries, of which the Certosa situla from Bologna is the finest example. Deterioration sets in by the fourth century when situlae such as the one from Boldu Dolfin, with its frieze of rather awkward animals, were produced.

A general consideration of the subjects portrayed in situla art must take into account the whole series of finds in this style from those as far afield as Kuffarn in Austria to the Certosa situla in Bologna.

A favourite motif was the procession of warriors marching in file, sometimes interspersed with charioteers and occasionally, as in the case of the Benvenuti situla, leading bound prisoners. Sporting scenes are another recurrent theme, with chariot-racing and boxing clearly rep-resented. In the boxing scenes the contestants are often shown with the prize, usually a helmet or a bronze vessel, behind them. We find, too, vignettes of everyday life, the ploughman carrying his plough back from

Fig. 65 Situla Art on belt plates. Far left, Este; left, Valle Trebba cemetery at Spina

the fields, a man netting rabbits, deer-hunting and scenes of basic entertainments such as drinking bouts, banqueting, musicians playing on the lyre and pipes, perhaps in competition, and very explicit pictures of love-making.

It has been suggested that these situlae were made especially for funerals and that the scenes are ritual in character, the sporting scenes being funerary games and the banquets funeral feasts. Such an interpretation is, however, questionable and they were probably used as wine containers before their secondary use as cremation urns, their decoration comprising themes aimed at catching the eye of the inebriated party guest.

The prehistorian is immediately attracted by the many details on these vessels which supplement the usual archaeological record. The plough, for example, which is not so different from the Bronze Age example from Ledro; also articles of clothing, the broad hats of the men and the shawled ladies, with their long floor-length dresses. Squads of soldiers on the same vessel are often attired in different types of helmets and shields, which could be seen as representing contingents from different tribes. The main armament of these warriors is the spear, but among them we also find small units of axe-men. The drinking equipment with situlate buckets and ladles is reminiscent of the sets of vessels found in Late Urnfield graves north of the Alps and indeed in the Golasecca grave at Ca' Morta. Furniture is frequently shown, high-backed chairs, beds and elaborate couches on which we can recognize an interesting combination of bird-ornamented panels along the backs, which suggest a connection with the Central European Urnfield bird motif; and beast-shaped headposts with limbs dangling from their mouths, which are of eastern Mediterranean inspiration.

This type of carved settee neatly summarizes the origin of situla art which can be best explained in terms of skilled local metalworkers, rooted in Urnfield culture technology, adopting and adapting the eastern Mediterranean Orientalizing motifs which arrived in the Veneto probably partly through Etruria but probably also through direct contact with the countries to the east. The art that developed out of these two sources of inspiration was, however, entirely local and the people portrayed on the situlae are without a doubt the local Iron Age population.

Other Este metalwork is fairly varied. In spite of the warlike scenes on the situlae few weapons have been found in graves. Antennae-hilted bronze swords were used during period II and there is a fine example of an iron sword with a bronze hilt of late eighth-century date from the cemetery below the Forte di Rivoli. During the sixth century short single-edged iron swords came into fashion.

Fig. 61, h

Besides lunate razors, knives and other utensils, we may mention the fine local tradition of bronze figurines which seem to have been mainly produced as votive offerings during the third and fourth phases. Some of these represent rather stylized horsemen and warriors but there are also some more naturalistic figures which include a lady in the folk costume of high boots, dress and tall cap. The bronze figures were undoubtedly inspired by Etruscan prototypes imported through the port of Adria.

Plates 57, 59

Plate 58

There are several shrines dating to the later periods of the Este culture which tell us all we know about the religious beliefs of these people. Three shrines have been found at Este itself and at least six more are recorded from other parts of the Este culture area. These sites are recognizable mainly by their associated votive deposits, which contain bronze statuettes of men, women and horses and votive inscriptions embossed on metal plaques. The dedications sometimes mention the name Reitia, a goddess who seems to have possessed healing powers, and the foundations of one of her temples were found at Fondo Baratela at Este. Embossed metal plaques probably depicting the same goddess holding a key were found further north at Montebelluna, while a hoard of gold plaques embossed with figures indicates another shrine in the centre of Vicenza. A large deposit of votive figures and some 3,500 small clay vessels were also recovered from the hot spring at San Pietro Montagnon in the Euganean Hills, where the waters are still considered to have medicinal powers.

Inscriptions on these votive offerings and on tombstones are written in a script derived mainly from Etruscan. The language itself however, unlike Etruscan, was clearly Indo-European and as recent studies have shown, was more closely related to Latin than any other tongue spoken in Italy at that time. Its similarity to Latin was possibly one reason for the rapidity with which Latin replaced Venetic once the Romans had arrived and, also, for the close friendship that always existed between these two peoples.

The first evidence of contact between Este and the eastern Mediterranean is found at the end of period II during the early sixth century. It is then that the Orientalizing elements of the situla occur, as well as direct imports such as a Greek Proto-Corinthian pot, a series of 18 little Egyptian-style faience figures, and beads of Red Sea coral. On the other hand, the establishment of a port at Adria in the late sixth century seems to have had little effect on the Este culture, judging by the few southern imports reaching Este during the fifth century.

Fig. 64, b

In the fourth century the Este culture came increasingly under the influence of the Celtic peoples who had by then established their dominance over the rest of the Po Plain. The Veneti in fact adopted so many Celtic traits at this time, that when Polybius described the Veneti of the second century BC he claimed that they were almost indistinguishable from the Celts in all but their language. Eventually, after a long alliance with Rome, the Veneti peacefully accepted the political control from there in 182 BC, which resulted in the total Romanization of their culture by the end of the millennium.

We cannot leave the Veneti without mentioning their eastern neighbours in the Julian Alps, who were mainly centred on the River Soča (Isonzo) and who controlled the eastern passes into Central Europe. The principal evidence for this group comes from the vast cemetery excavated by Marchesetti at Santa Lucia at the end of the last century. Whether these people should be called Veneti or Illyrians it is difficult to say, but again, as through so much of North Italian prehistory, this flourishing enclave demonstrates the close relationship between the cultures of the North Italian Plain and Central Europe.

Skirting the eastern limit of the Plain, in the provinces of Udine and Gorizia and along the natural eastern frontier of Italy, are to be found a number of fortifications. Some are situated on low ground, with rectangular banks and ditches, and others are on hill-tops, but few have been excavated. One at Gradisca has however produced Este-type fibulae.

THE CASTELLIERI OF TRIESTE

From the Middle Bronze Age onwards, the main axis of communication between the Italian Plain and the Danube river system was across the Predil pass and the Julian Alps. South of this line we can recognize the presence of a more conservative and isolated cultural region which was occupied by the Istri at the time of the Roman Conquest, and probably by the ancestors of this tribe in the Iron Age and the Bronze Age. The principal monuments which these people have left to posterity are the *castellieri*, hill-forts, of which many thousands are known. They cluster almost exclusively on the barren limestone Karst hills and reach their northerly distribution at Redipuglia, where the Karst itself ends.

Fig. 66
Plate 63

Every small community had its own massive defences constructed of boulders of limestone. There appear to be three main variations in fortress plan; those with double, separated ramparts, which form an inner and an outer enclosure; the cliff-castle type defended by a semi-circular rampart on one side and a steep cliff on the other; and the contour fort. Animals bones from some sites suggest that sheep were the basic livestock but red deer were also hunted in large numbers.

Fig. 66   Characteristic Castelliere plans from the Karst. Left, double enclosure at Redipuglia; right, cliff castle at Doberdo

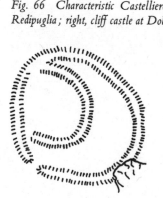
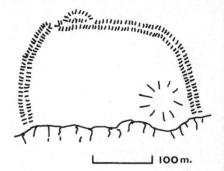

100 m.

The *castellieri* pottery is extremely crude and massive, and pots are often provided with ornamental elbow handles whose ancestry can be traced back to the Early Bronze Age. Tripod pots and clay rings for standing pots on were other distinctive objects. A small hollow-based flint arrow-head was in use for hunting and warfare.

The lack of metalwork on these sites and their isolation from the main stream of cultural development makes the dating of the *castellieri* a considerable problem. At present we can only assume some sort of direct continuity from the Middle Bronze Age to the time when the last strongholds of the Histri were besieged by the Roman legions.

THE GOLASECCA CULTURE AND ITS WARRIOR CHIEFTAINS

Our knowledge of the Early Iron Age peoples of Lombardy, like those of Bologna and Este, is derived almost entirely from the excavation of cemeteries. These have been found in considerable numbers concentrated in the area of the Western Alpine lakes between Novara and Bergamo and, to judge from their distribution, the lakes of Maggiore and Como must have been the focal points in the development of this third North Italian Iron Age culture of Golasecca.

The Golasecca culture is not an entirely homogeneous phenomenon, for marked regional differences manifest themselves in pottery and burial custom. These discrepancies led Randall MacIver in 1927 to propose that the term Golasecca should be restricted to the cemeteries on the River Ticino immediately to the south of Lake Maggiore while other cemetery groups should have other regional names (Comacine for the Como region, etc.). Randall MacIver's suggestion has not been generally accepted, since as yet these regional variations have not been satisfactorily defined and in spite of this diversity the whole area does seem to share a certain common heritage.

Regional concentrations of the Golasecca culture can be recognized in the Ticino valley south of Lake Maggiore (Golasecca, Castelletto Ticino, Sesto Calende), in the Novara region of Piedmont (Ameno, San Bernardino di Briona), round Lake Varese (Cunardo, Castello, Val Travaglia), Lake Como (Ca' Morta, Albate, Civiglio, Grandate, Rebato, etc.); and there was another nucleus round Bellinzona to the north of Lake Maggiore. Outside this obvious cultural homeland, Golasecca finds are few and far between. Golasecca burials are known

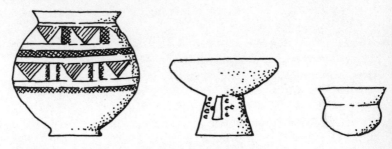

Fig. 67   Golasecca I pottery from Ca' Morta

for example in the Val Camonica (Breno), while to the south-west the cemeteries in the Stura valley round Cuneo are best considered with the Ligurian culture area rather than with Golasecca.

A firm chronological framework for the development of the Golasecca culture was worked out by Pompeo Castelfranco, the Lombard pre-historian who excavated a large number of cemeteries between 1870 and 1880. His scheme of three main phases, based on an intimate knowledge of the pottery and fibulae from the sites he investigated has stood the test of time, although now revised and subdivided by the more recent studies carried out by de Marinis and Renato Peroni. The three stages can be dated as follows: Golasecca I, 900–600; Golasecca II, 600–450; and Golasecca III, 450–15 BC.

The scattered cemeteries consist of areas of inurned cremations containing tens, hundreds or in the case of sites like Ca' Morta and Golasecca, even thousands of burials.

At Golasecca itself, the basic burial custom shows little change through more than 500 years. The urns were normally put in pits lined with pebbles or stone slabs during Golasecca I, while proper rectangular stone cists are standard in the Golasecca II period, and finally in Golasecca III inhumation makes its appearance alongside cremation.

Tomb structure, however, varied regionally. In the Novara group, tumulus mounds are found containing single or multiple burials and around Bellinzona, graves are sometimes covered by stone cairns. At Ameno (Lortallo) urns were clustered into groups which perhaps represent family burial plots, while in the same cemetery we find enclosures and alignments marking the graves. South of Maggiore there are also a number of graves marked in a similar manner with circles and rectangles of large glacial boulders. These occur at Monsorino and in the area between Somma and Vergiate, while a keyhole-shaped enclosure, which combines in its plan a circle and a rectangle, is recorded at Somma. Gravestones carved into a stylized anthropomorphic shape, with a disc head and narrow body, and inscribed in the local Etruscan script (Lepontian) appear rarely during the final stages of Golasecca.

With the majority of the burials the grave goods are monotonously uniform, comprising an urn, usually with a bowl over it for a lid, and a number of accessory pots. Besides the pottery the most usual object put in the grave was a fibula, other objects such as bracelets, lance-heads and knives being exceptional.

There are, however, a few graves whose wealth and warlike apparel is in complete contrast with the usual Golasecca style of burials. The social implication of these tombs is of special interest since they could be interpreted as the graves of chieftains honoured in their capacity as war leaders, and thus indicate a social structure completely different from that of Bologna or Este.

The latest research shows that Golasecca I (900–600 BC) can be divided into three sub-phases. The earliest graves are from the Mesma cemetery at Ameno on Lake Orta and from Moncucco (Como). Both sites show evidence of the descent of the Golasecca tradition from cultures of the out-going Bronze Age, since Mesma produced arc fibulae and pottery decorated with 'false-cord' impression and at Moncucco a Golasecca urn was found with an intentionally broken bronze sword, bracelets and a bronze spear-head, all of which hark back to the tradition of Canegrate.

The pottery of the period is characterized by well-rounded urns with everted rims which are decorated with incised hatched triangles and bands. Small rounded cups are used as accessory vessels. Leech- and boat-shaped fibulae are usual.

Fig. 67

It is during this phase that the earliest of the series of rich chieftain burials was interred, at Ca' Morta (Como). This contained a whole series of metal objects, a socketed bronze axe, an iron-tipped spear, and a beaten-bronze drinking service, comprising ribbed cups, a ladle and an amphora decorated with embossed designs which incorporated the Urnfield motif of the 'sun-boat and swan'. There was also a bronze bowl decorated with bronze pendants set on a wheeled trolley, which is a type of vessel that has parallels among the Late Urnfield cultures of Central and Northern Europe (Milavec, Bohemia; Peccatel, Germany; and Skallerup, Denmark). The traces of a larger wheeled vehicle were also noticed, a possibility which is backed up by the presence of a horse-bit.

In a detailed study of the Ca' Morta burial, Kossak has demonstrated how practically all the features of this burial, the drinking equipment, the cauldron cart, the horse-bit, the larger waggon and even the combination of a spear and an axe as armaments are all to be paralleled in the final Urnfield culture (Hallstatt B) and the first stage of the Iron Age (Hallstatt C) to the north and east of the Alps, which would date the tomb to about 700 B C.

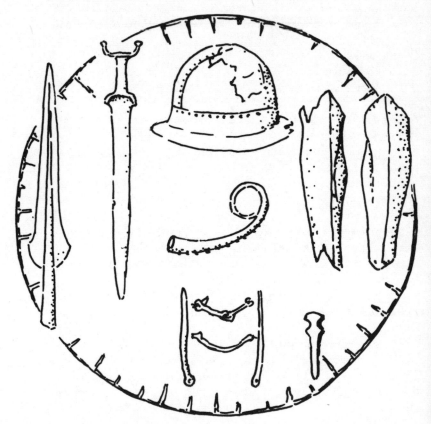

Two chariot burials from Sesto Calende at the southern end of Lake Maggiore belong to a later moment in the evolution of Golasecca I. Tomb A, at Sesto Calende, discovered in 1867, consisted of an inurned cremation, set in a six-foot-deep pit, and covered by a cairn of stones. The accompanying grave goods comprised three accessory pots, a bronze situla decorated with men and animals drawn in outline with repoussée dots, an iron sword with an antennae hilt and bronze sheath, an iron lance- and arrow-heads, a bronze helmet with a broad brim, and two bronze greaves. There were also the remains of a two-wheeled chariot or cart represented by two iron tyres, iron lynch-pins and two curved, hollow bronze horns which may have served as hand-holds for mounting the vehicle. Two horse-bits completed the collection.

Tomb B, found in 1927, contained similar finds also under a cairn of stones. There were 22 pots, some decorated with pattern burnish, another bronze situla with crude embossed figure decoration, a cylindrical bronze bucket with widely spaced horizontal ribs of the type which is characteristic of the Arnoaldi phase at Bologna, and a small four-wheeled cauldron cart, carrying a bronze bowl set on a central column and adorned with small jangling pendants. Again, armaments comprise an iron sword with antennae hilt and an iron spear, together with a bronze helmet with a crest fitting, and leg greaves. The iron tyres and lynch-pins

Fig. 68

Fig. 69

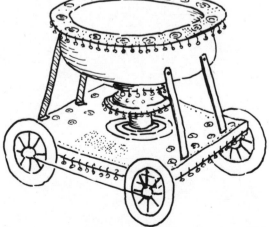

Fig. 68 Metal goods from grave A at Sesto Calende. Diameter of tyre 84 cm.

Fig. 69 Reconstructed cauldron cart from tomb B at Sesto Calende. Height 26 cm.

Fig. 70 Golasecca II pottery from Ca' Morta

of another two-wheeled chariot and the metal parts of bridle and harness were also recovered. Roughly contemporary with the Sesto Calende warriors are two burials with similar swords and brimmed helmets from the San Bernardino di Briona cemetery (Novara).

The date of the Sesto Calende burials has been the subject of debate for more than a century and only recently has H. O. Frey been able to show conclusively that the armaments find their closest parallels in the burials of the Hallstatt C warriors of the seventh century in the Alps. The Hallstatt C burial at Vace in Slovenia, with its brimmed helmet and antennae sword is strikingly similar, while to the west a burial at Mailhac in Provence produced a chariot and comparable grave goods.

Although vehicle burial was practised north of the Alps in Late Urnfield times (as at Hart in Bavaria) it is perhaps to seventh-century Etruria (Vetulonia) that we should turn for two-wheeled chariots comparable to those found at Sesto Calende, for waggon burial only becomes common north of the Alps in the late sixth century and chariot burials are not found there until the La Tène period.

Fig. 70

In the Golasecca II period (600–450) more elegant, pear-shaped urns and open bowls with low feet come into fashion in the Ticino valley. Both these forms are usually decorated with pattern-burnished designs of bands and cross hatching. In the Como region, however, during the same period a shouldered situlate urn is the rule and pattern-burnishing is rare.

Besides this standard pottery we occasionally find red- and black-banded pots, inspired by the Este III pottery of the Veneto, as well as a variety of more exotic ceramic products. A special technique of pot

decoration using applied metal foil, introduced perhaps from Switzerland, and black graphite and red paint was sometimes used. Stamped
ornament of the type in vogue during the Arnoaldi phase in Bologna,
with circles, rosettes and 's' motifs was applied to some situlate urns and
to double-branched candelabra-like incense burners at Ca' Morta. These
incense vessels have detachable bowls in which aromatic resin was found
still preserved. Curious bird-shaped pots from Ca' Morta, Sesto Calende
and Albate belong to the same series of bird-shaped vessels as the Este
bird discussed on p. oo.

Plate 62

Plate 61

Apart from leech and serpentine fibulae, which now, in keeping with
the general North Italian pattern, develop elongated catch-plates, and a
few sheet-bronze belt plates, metal objects in graves are rare. Isolated
examples of situla art, like the lid from Rebato decorated with a fine
frieze of animals, are probably imports from the Veneto. The over-all
impression is of a metal technology less advanced than that found in the
more urbanized centres of Bologna and Este.

A fourth 'chieftain's' grave, again from Ca' Morta, can be dated to the
end of Golasecca II. Its principle feature was a four-wheeled vehicle,
which this time bears a very striking resemblance to the waggon burials
of the Late Hallstatt period beyond the Alps. The wheel hubs sheathed
with metal, the balustrades and the repoussée-decorated bronze panels
from the sides of the carriage are almost identical with the metal parts of
the waggons from burials in France at Vix and Ohnenheim, Alsace,
or Hochmichele in Germany. Whereas few of the Hallstatt waggons
are later than 500 B C, the Ca' Morta vehicle was buried at about the
middle of the fifth century since, besides an Etruscan bronze beaked
flagon and a Certosa fibula, it was accompanied by an imported Attic
red-figure cup datable to the early fifth century.

Plate 60

Who then were these chosen few out of the thousands buried in the
urnfields around the Lombard lakes? Does the presence of these warrior
graves with their transalpine connections help to explain the gradual
Celtic infiltration of the area at the end of the fifth century? Answers to
these questions must await further discoveries and research.

During the fifth century Lombardy was clearly developing trade
contacts with the Etruscan and Greek worlds, as we can see, for example,
from the imports in the Ca' Morta burial. Etruscan flagons, made in
Vulci like the one from the Ca' Morta burial, turn up also in the

Bellinzona cemeteries in the Swiss Ticino valley and the same objects were now traded across the Alpine passes, probably the Simplon and the San Bernardino, to the La Tène aristocracy of France and Germany.

Evidence of this Alpine trade with Golasecca is also to be noticed in the pottery styles of Hallstatt settlements, like Mont Lassois on the Seine, for here stamp-decorated wares are found, as well as elegant forms comparable to those of Golasecca II which perhaps inspired the develop-ment of the distinctive La Tène pottery.

During Golasecca III (450–15 BC) the Celtic La Tène style first appeared in Lombardy and we are faced with the complex problem of distinguishing the local Golaseccan from the intrusive Celtic culture.

Golasecca III has been divided by Bertolone and Crivelli into three subdivisions A, B and C. In Golasecca III A (450–350) the local pottery tradition is radically changed by the introduction of the potter's wheel and classical prototypes. The latter include copies of the Etruscan

Fig. 71

metal-spouted flagons which we have seen at Ca' Morta. Other distinc-tive vessels in this phase are the two-tiered conical beakers which are often decorated with little stamped patterns, rosettes, circles, and even horses

Fig. 62, b

and birds, a technique perhaps carried over from Golasecca II. We also find shallow bowls of classical inspiration, single-handled jars, and mortaria mixing bowls.

Fig. 80

In Golasecca III B (320–250) the pear-shaped beaker replaces the conical one and a distinctive narrow-necked peg-top bottle (*olpe*) first makes its appearance and continues as a popular local pot form through into Roman times. In metalwork Certosa fibulae are still produced and even late versions of long-footed leech fibulae survive. The latter are provided with enormous cast-metal balls on the end of the catch-plates. Celtic-style La Tène metal objects, swords and fibulae are now not uncommon in graves, and Golasecca becomes increasingly celticized.

How far we can in fact talk of a Golasecca culture after this phase is a matter of debate, in view of the increasing Celtic penetration. What was actually involved in the Celtic take-over of Lombardy is not at all clear, and is a problem discussed more fully in the next chapter.

Roman influence, in addition to continuing La Tène elements, is the hall-mark of Golasecca III C. From about 200 BC the first glossy black pottery bowls, known as Campanian ware, were imported into Lombardy. This distinctive pottery was probably manufactured in the

Fig. 71 Golasecca III A pottery. Left, Ca' Morta; right, Rebbio

Roman colonies of Rimini, Piacenza and Cremona. The Roman armies in fact penetrated to the heart of Golasecca territory as early as 196 BC, when an army under Marcellus captured Como. Complete romanization of the area was, however, a slow process and native and Celtic features survive down to the final subjugation of the area in 15 BC.

A local dialect, which philologists call Lepontian, written in a northern variant of the Etruscan alphabet, was in use in the area between the lakes of Orta and Como just prior to the Roman Conquest. Although texts in Lepontian are short, scarce and not easily decipherable, grammatical features are recognizable which have led Joshua Whatmough to claim that it is a native Italian language showing considerable Celtic influence. He called it Celto-Ligurian. More recently, G. B. Pellegrini has suggested that it is in fact a language closely related to Celtic. In either case it is interesting to note that the language reflects the same mixture of Celtic and native traits recognizable in the material archaeological remains. Little wonder that the classical historians were undecided as to whether the Lepontii, the Comenses and the Orobii, who inhabited the region of the Lombard lakes at the time of the Roman Conquest, were Celts or local Raeti.

We have few details about the settlements of the Golaseccan people, perhaps partly due to an over-indulgence in cemetery excavation. Those sites that have been located include low-lying settlements like Merlotitt on the tributary of the Ticino and the reoccupied site of the Neolithic village of Isolino on Lake Varese. In another village, Rondineto (Como) occupied during Golasecca II and III, rectangular rock-cut hut foundations have been recorded. There are settlements too in naturally defended positions and even proper hill-forts, the best documented of which is the Caslé di Ramponio, on a summit 3,423 ft above Lake

Lugano. At the Caslé some 19,000 sq. yds were enclosed by a single wall of rampart, and square hut foundations were found sunk below ground level behind the northern embankment.

These settlements also produced, besides the characteristic Golasecca pottery, large quantities of coarse ware of a type little known in the cemeteries. This mainly comprised shouldered, situlate pots, with slightly splayed rims and decorated lines of impressions or slashes on the rims and shoulders.

THE IRON AGE IN THE CENTRAL ALPINE VALLEYS

Soon after 1000 B C we find an Iron Age culture taking shape in a mountain territory which encompasses a large part of eastern Switzerland as far north as Lake Constance, and the Italian areas of the Alto Adige (South Tyrol), the province of Trento, and the Camonica and Tellina valleys.

The archaeological record of this region down to the final conquest of the Central Alps by the Romans in 15 B C can be seen as a continuous development of a rather conservative mountain population. Pre-historians have divided this evolution into two main phases on the basis mainly of pottery styles, namely the Melaun-Laugen (Meluno-Luco) period (900–400 B C) and the San Zeno phase (400–15 B C).

The earliest stages of the Melaun-Laugen phase are best represented in the extensive and long-lived cremation cemetery at Vadena (Pfatten) south of Bolzano. Some of the early graves at Vadena can be clearly correlated with the start of Este, Bologna and Golasecca to the south. The

Fig. 72 San Zeno pottery from Montesei (Trento)

Vadena urns are usually much squatter in shape than those of the Po Valley, and they are decorated with geometric patterns executed with incision, 'false-cord' and dot impressions. In the metalwork we find close parallels with both the Alpine cultures of the Austrian Tyrol and the centres of Bologna and Este during the ninth and eighth centuries BC. There are for example, lunate razors, hump-backed tanged knives, thick bowed and leech fibulae. A fine bronze horse-bit with terminals cast in the shape of horses provides us with a direct link with Bologna while a whole series of embossed bronze discs can probably be interpreted as harness ornaments.

The local Laugen (Luco) and Melaun (Meluno) pottery styles are also present at Vadena. In both cases the principal pottery vessel involved is an odd-looking jug, which has a splayed base, everted rim and long rim-to-base handle. The Laugen-style vessel is apparently the earlier over most of the Central Alpine region and is also the more elaborate. The *Fig. 73* rim is decorated with multiple peaks and carefully impressed rope moulding along the edge. A common feature also is the pair of bosses (breasts?) to the front of the vessel which are enclosed by a semicircular festoon. Surface decoration in the form of bands of incised, grooved, herring-bone motifs and impressed dots are also usual. The Melaun jug is a simpler version of the Laugen form, usually just having a triangular peak, strengthened by a verical rib on the rim opposite the handle and a minimum of decoration in the shape of a cordon festoon on the front. The Melaun pottery has a more restricted distribution than the Laugen and appears to be a late northern version of the former. In the cemetery of Melaun itself this pottery was found associated with Certosa fibulae of the fifth century BC.

During the fifth century the second main pottery tradition, the San *Fig. 72* Zeno style came into vogue. The most distinctive ceramic products of the San Zeno period were the small but wide rounded bowls, which were probably used as drinking cups. The base of these bowls always has a large central boss – the so-called omphalos base – and their surface is always decorated with impressed designs. These impressions were usually done with a broad comb-like instrument which produced a vertical milled line, or else with stamps with carved concentric circles, stars, and *Fig. 62, d* other motifs. It is interesting to find here the technique of stamped impressions which was first popular in the Arnoaldi phase at Bologna and later spread to Golasecca, Este and eventually to the early La Tène culture north of the Alps.

Apart from its pottery, this Alpine culture possessed little that was not borrowed from other neighbouring peoples, firstly during the Melaun-Laugen phase from Este and the other Iron Age cultures of the Po Valley, and later during the San Zeno phase from Este and the Celts.

The influence of Este is especially strong during the fifth century, when we find a local school of situla art established in the Adige valley; at about the same time an alphabet was introduced (the Bolzano alphabet), which uses characters clearly borrowed from the Venetic script. Inscriptions in this alphabet mainly take the form of brief votive dedications inscribed on pieces of antler, strips of wood or even on bronze figurines.

Added to the influence of the Este culture from the fourth century onwards is the influx of Celtic La Tène-style objects. In fact the majority of objects in bronze and iron – swords, spears, fibulae, etc. – found associated with San Zeno pottery are La Tène in design. There is indeed some historical evidence to suggest some sort of Celtic penetration of the area, for Trento itself is claimed by some ancient writers to have been founded by the Celts. However, even though some Celts may have come into the region, perhaps as blacksmiths and metalworkers, the bulk of the population were almost certainly of indigenous descent and can be identified with the people the Romans knew as the Raeti.

Continuity of settlement from Melaun-Laugen through into the San Zeno phase is demonstrated, for example, at Montesei (Trento) and Monte Ozol (Trento), both of which showed San Zeno material stratified above levels containing Laugen pottery. This continued use of the same settlement, as well as the survival of the handled jug as a popular vessel, is evidence of an enduring local population.

Pliny and Livy and other Roman writers have left us the legend that the Raeti were descended from remnants of the Etruscan settlers of the Po Valley who took refuge in the Alps at the time of the Celtic invasions. Archaeological backing for this account is, however, meagre to say the least. Even if a band of Etruscans did flee to these mountain valleys at the end of the fifth century, they must have been quickly absorbed by the local population along with the numerous Celtic and Venetic craftsmen and traders who were setting up their workshops and trading posts along the Adige and its tributaries at this time.

Fig. 73 Jug with a spout and ornamental handle of the Laugen (Luco) type. Museo Trentino di Storia Naturale, Trento

Settlement sites are even more numerous in the Alpine valleys during the Iron Age than in the Bronze Age Plabach culture, again usually found on hill-top sites, with or without artificial defences. More than 700 hill-forts have in fact been recorded in the South Tyrol by G. Innerebner of Bolzano in recent years, a large proportion of which can be assumed to be Iron Age in date even though dating evidence and excavation has been scarce. A large number of hill settlements has similarly been recognized in the province of Trento.

Most of these sites could have been little more than fortified farmsteads since they are seldom more than 50 yards in diameter. Their defences, when present, consist of rough stone ramparts, which make the best use of the natural slopes for protection. Additional evidence of structural refinements in these fortifications includes the presence of double ramparts on several sites and a long narrow corridor entrance, projecting beyond the line of the defences, on the Jobenbühel (Bolzano).

Some of these settlements lie at a considerable altitude. Two hill-forts on the plateau of the Schlern (Sciliar) mountain in the Dolomites, at a height of about 8,200 feet, may have been used as summer camps for shepherds and cattle herders. Professor G. Leonardi, who excavated these sites, maintains however that one of them, Monte Castello-Burgstall, which produced Laugen pottery, was too inaccessible to have been anything other than a religious sanctuary. A look-out post might be an alternative explanation.

Well-preserved house foundations have been found on some sites of the San Zeno period. Rectangular stone footings for houses with wooden

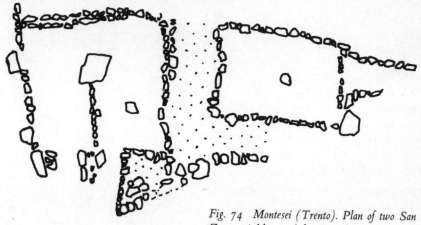

Fig. 74 Montesei (Trento). Plan of two San Zeno period houses (after Perini). 1 : 200

Fig. 74

superstructures were excavated within the ramparts of the hill-fort of Bellamonte (Trento), while similar rectangular but semi-subterranean house cellars are known from other sites. At Montesei (Trento) two houses have been excavated measuring 23 by 14 feet and 23 by 22 feet 3 inches respectively. These had stone walls set some 3 feet below ground level and a centrally placed stone for a roof support. A double entrance, on the short side, was approached by a ramp. A larger complex was excavated in the Val di Non at the type site San Zeno, where similar sunken foundations have entrance wells containing stone stairways. Here traces of the house's wooden superstructure were noted 31½ inches up the stone foundation wall. The houses at San Zeno produced a remarkable quantity of metalwork; apart from Certosa fibulae, most of it was of Celtic La Tène style and included swords, spears, helmets, fire-dogs, fibulae and smithing equipment. Finally we can mention a waterlogged wooden subterranean cellar, built in log cabin fashion, on the hill of Collalbo-Klobstein above Bolzano.

To the south of the main Melaun-San Zeno area in the Lessini Mountains, just north of Verona, is a whole series of late Iron Age hill-forts which lie in the border zone between the territories of Este and San Zeno and there is thus some uncertainty as to whether their inhabitants were Veneti, Raeti or even perhaps Celts.

A number of features of the San Zeno tradition are, however, found on these sites and the cellared type of rectangular house that we have seen in the Trento region is represented here at Monte Loffa, where shallow cellars were cut into the limestone rock, the walls being lined with vertical slabs of stone. In one of these basements, 49 loom weights were found, in the exact position where a loom had been abandoned two thousand years ago. A more carefully built small hill-fort was excavated not far away from Monte Loffa at Sottosengia. It has a roughly rectangular rampart, built of dry stone walling, which surrounds three sides, while the fourth is defended by a sheer cliff. Rectangular rooms, built with blocks of limestone and paved with flat slabs, back up against this rampart, leaving an open court in the centre. Access to the inside courtyard appears to have been by means of a stairway leading up on to the perimeter wall and down again inside it. A row of loom weights was found in one of the rooms at this site too.

Fig. 75

Fig. 75   Plan of the small fortified settlement of Sottosengia (Verona). Rooms are arranged backing up against the well-built rampart wall

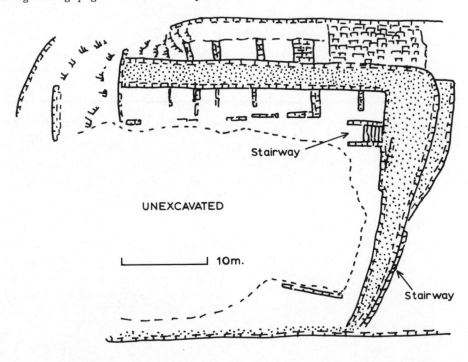

Stairway

UNEXCAVATED

10m.

Stairway

Plate 68

In the province of Trento and the Alto Adige and Tyrol we find Este-style sanctuaries with associated votive deposits. One of these is at Moritzing (S. Maurizio), near Bolzano, where a well was excavated containing 5,000 bronze rings and some Certosa fibulae. A large and varied collection of votive objects was also recovered from house C at San Zeno, which also seems to have been some kind of a shrine. Little bronze horses, fish, crabs, a dolphin and human figures were all found here, some carrying inscribed dedications in the Bolzano script. Short inscriptions of a similar votive type have been found at San Zeno, Montesei, Meclo-Mechel, Appiano-Eppan and other sites in the Adige valley; they are carved on pieces of deer antler, or on birch bark like those from the waterlogged farmstead at Collalbo-Klobstein (Bolzano).

The tradition of drawing on rock surfaces in the nearby Val Camonica survived well into the Iron Age, and underwent a great rejuvenation at this time (Anati's period IV in the development of Camunian art). In contrast with the religious overtones of the Bronze Age engravings the rock artists were now mainly concerned with scenes of everyday life. Represented are ox-drawn waggons, women at the loom, the smith at his forge and houses. Just as popular, if not more so, were the heroic scenes of single combat between helmeted warriors on foot or horseback, fighting with spear or leaf-shaped sword. Anati also attributes scenes of stags to this late period and even goes as far as to suggest the existence of a stag cult. The occasional inscription in local north Etruscan script is found on some rocks, confirming a date after 500 BC for some of these engravings. Drawings of sword-bearing warriors at Punta San Virgilio on Lake Garda are probably also of this date.

Back in the Adige valley, rocks with cup markings were found closely associated with one of the San Zeno houses at Montesei and curious grooved and pitted pebbles have been found here and at other sites. All are phenomena which at present are difficult to explain.

The end of many of the settlements that have been excavated appears to have been violent and coincides in many cases with the arrival of the Romans at the end of the first century BC. San Zeno and the Dos de Arca (Val Camonica) were destroyed by fire at this time and the coin evidence from Sottosengia ends with early Roman denarii. It is tempting to correlate these events with the Alpine campaign of Drusus when he subdued the Raetian mountaineers in their strongholds in 15 BC.

According to classical tradition the Ligurians were an ancient indigenous race who formerly occupied a much wider territory than that which has inherited their name. To the west, the coast of southern France up to the Rhône was inhabited by them before the arrival of the Celts, the Greek colony of Massalia (Marseilles) itself being founded in Ligurian territory. Eastwards it was said that the whole western part of the Po Plain had belonged to the Ligurians, again before the Celtic inroads.

The identification of a Ligurian archaeological culture corresponding to this wider area is, however, difficult. In the past, attempts have been made to equate the Neolithic and the Terremare peoples of the north with the ancient Ligurians and although this kind of speculation in respect of the remoter periods of prehistory has proved rather fruitless, the possibility that the Golasecca culture represents one aspect of this original Ligurian culture has greater credibility.

Following the Celtic penetration of Lombardy, we find in Piedmont a number of tribes who were apparently of mixed stock. The Taurini, for example, are called Celts by Polybius and Ligurians by Pliny, while Strabo uses the term Celto-Ligurian for many of the tribes along the Western Alps. Although Strabo has been accused of imprecision by philologists and historians, the term Celto-Ligurian probably most objectively reflects the process of native acculturation by the Celts that we can see in the archaeological record and which we have already mentioned in connection with Golasecca III.

In this chapter we shall limit our description of the Ligurians to those areas which were still called Ligurian at the time of their first contacts with Rome, namely the present-day Ligurian coast, south-western Piedmont and the northern Apennines.

The Roman armies took some two hundred years to conquer the wild Ligurian tribes and used their lands virtually as training grounds for the legions. These continuous Ligurian wars perhaps explain the rather dismal accounts that Posidonius gives of the Ligurians for he describes them as living on the margin of survival in caves and poorly-made huts of reeds or wood. He writes too that agriculture was difficult and that they existed chiefly by hunting, as well as mentioning their beer and their use of the sling in warfare.

Strabo paints a slightly rosier picture of the Ligurians and records that their economy was based on herd animals and that they produced honey, timber and hides. The Ligurians who inhabited the coast were also renowned in antiquity for their seamanship and piracy.

The archaeological evidence suggests a division between the more prosperous coastal dwellers whose orientation was towards the sea and trade, on the one hand, and the more backward mountain folk living in hill-forts in the interior, on the other.

On the Ligurian coast evidence has now been found of a relatively rich local Iron Age cultural development running parallel to the Iron Age of Golasecca, Bologna and Este, although unfortunately the sequence is not as yet completely documented all the way through. In 1959 Professor Lamboglia started the excavation on the cemetery of Chiavari and for the first time brought to light an early stage of the Ligurian Iron Age coastal culture dating to the eighth century B C.

Plate 64

The cemetery was laid out on ground that had been artificially levelled by dumping masses of pot wasters from the nearby kiln. Urns containing cremations were found here placed in cists made from slate slabs and these in turn were set in a patchwork of contiguous rectangular and circular enclosures constructed from similar slabs of slate, somewhat reminiscent of the circle graves of seventh-century Etruria or some of the cemeteries in Este. The enclosures were presumably for individual family burials since each had a central interment with additional later burials surrounding it. The urns mostly had a plain globular body and a

Fig. 76

cylindrical neck, but were made in a great variety of wares and were decorated with all manner of different techniques and designs. These latter include the use of red and white paint, stamped designs (with

Fig. 62, c

horses, human figures and abstract patterns) and applied relief decoration using ribs and even moulded animals (snakes and lizards).

Evidence of a local folk costume for women, different from that of any other North Italian Iron Age group, is to be seen in the recurrent finds in female graves of metal arm-rings on each arm, a special type of

Fig. 77

rectangular studded belt plate and traces of leather garments also covered with large bronze studs. The fibulae on the other hand are of the more 'international' long-footed leech, boat and serpentine types. The menfolk were buried together with lunate bronze razors like those found in the Benacci cemetery at Bologna but sometimes they had iron spears and daggers as well, which contrast with the usually weapon-free burials of the Po Plain.

Two centuries later than Chiavari, is the large cemetery at Genoa in use between about 475 and 325 BC. The graves now contain rich imported goods from the south, indicating the importance of Genoa as a port already during the centuries before the Roman invasion. The inventory of southern products includes Greek red-figure pottery, perfume jars of alabaster, glass vessels and bronze strygils for cleaning the body, Etuscan bronze ladles and flagons of bronze. The Certosa fibula and a La Tène sword and amber objects show other lines of contact.

The local pottery consisted of rounded urns, large mortaria mixing bowls with abrasive stone grit set into the inside surface, and buff-coloured flagons which copy the imported bronze prototypes. In some tombs wooden bowls as well as the wood plank coverings of the burial chambers had been preserved.

In contrast with the cosmopolitan coastal ports, the sites in the mountains of the Ligurian interior appear impoverished. Here the principal settlements are hill-forts, many of which may have been erected at the time of the wars with Rome. A good example is Monte Bignone behind San Remo where a promontory fort was provided with a sizable ditched defence. Excavations within the rampart here uncovered two well-built rectangular stone houses.

Plate 65

On the northern slopes of the Ligurian Alps in Piedmont are such hill-settlements as Rossiglione and Bec Berciassa. At the latter site cups and situlate pottery, with incised and finger-impressed decoration, have been found together with the bones of cattle, sheep and wild animals. A whole chain of little-studied hill-forts has also been identified along the crest of the northern Apennines in Emilia.

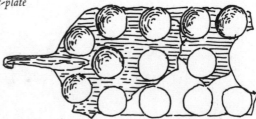

Figs 76, 77 Chiavari. Ligurian style urn and studded belt-plate

CHAPTER IX

Greeks, Celts and Romans in the Po Valley

SPINA, ADRIA AND GREEK TRADE

Fig. 59

One of the most spectacular archaeological finds in Italy this century has been the rediscovery of the ancient port of Spina on the Adriatic, some forty miles south of Venice. Classical writers record that the Spineti were the dominant maritime power in the Adriatic by the end of the sixth century B C and yet for nearly two thousand years the exact location of their city has remained a mystery. In 1922, however, a chance dis-covery led to the identification of the first of the rich cemeteries of the settlement and in 1956 the complete layout of the town itself, covering some 740 acres of land, was seen and photographed from the air.

Plate 73

On the remarkable series of photographs taken by Valvassori one can clearly distinguish the dark network of intersecting canals, the waterways of the old port, looking surprisingly like those still used in nearby Venice and Chioggia. Side canals connected with a main axial 'Grand Canal', which was possibly the main harbour area, while this, in turn linked the town to a long vanished estuary of the Po.

Limited excavations on one of the *insulae* of the town have revealed the remains of wooden piles and platforms, which had been put in to consolidate the ground beneath the houses.

Far more extensive are the excavations that have been carried out in the two cemeteries of Spina, in the Valle Trebba and the Valle Pega, where a total of more than 3,500 graves have so far been excavated. Here the burial rite was a mixture of inhumation and cremation, with the former slightly outnumbering the latter. The rich grave goods reflect a prosperous trading community, and gold ornaments, ear-rings and diadems, which were probably manufactured by the goldsmiths of the Greek colony of Taranto, are by no means uncommon. There is also an extensive collection of Attic red-figure pottery of fifth-century date, which has been one of the main attractions of Spina for the classical archae-ologist. Bronze vessels manufactured in Este and Etruria also feature

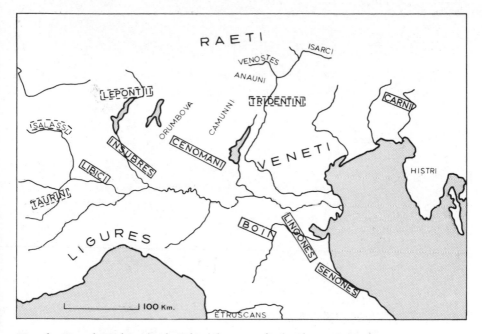

Fig. 78   Map of Cisalpine Gaul. Celtic tribes are outlined with a continuous line, tribes of mixed Celtic and native origin or with doubtful Celtic affiliations, with a dotted line

among the grave goods. All these finds provide us with a closely datable series of objects which show that the port was flourishing between about 530 and 300 BC.

Who, then, was responsible for the establishment of Spina? Ancient historians, as usual, present us with conflicting answers to this question and we find that Greeks, Etruscans and even Umbrians have in turn been held responsible for the foundation of the city.

The fact that the Spineti had their own treasury at Delphi might suggest that the Greeks dominated the community, and the large quantities of Greek pottery and occasional Greek *graffito* on the pottery would seem to support this idea. However, like all ports, its inhabitants must have been multi-racial and, if it is dangerous to assume the presence of Etruscans from Bologna or Veneti from Este on the evidence of the imported bronze vessels from these two centres, the *graffiti* in Etruscan on pottery are a stronger argument for the presence of inhabitants other than Greek.

Only about two hundred years after its foundation Spina was deserted. According to Dionysius of Halicarnassus it was destroyed by the Celts in about 300 B C. The reason why it never recovered after this setback, however, may well have been the silting-up of the harbour and the advance of the coastline eastwards, a fate which later befell Ravenna and its port of Classe.

Strabo recorded that the Etruscans were responsible for the building of canals and the first drainage operations in the marshy estuary of the River Po, while Pliny mentions an Etruscan canal which connected Spina with Adria, the port situated in the territory of the Veneti to the north of Spina.

Adria today is no more than a small sleepy provincial town in the eastern Po Plain, but in antiquity it was so important a port that it led to its name being used to describe the sea bordering the east coast of Italy.

According to Strabo, Adria was founded by the Veneti, but Livy and Pliny claimed it as one of the twelve Etruscan cities of the north while other writers have attributed its origin to Greek colonists. Whoever may have originally founded the town it is clear that, like Spina, it soon became a lively international port. Archaeological evidence in fact hints at the presence of all of the three ethnic groups mentioned above, although the clearest proof of any one group of peoples living in the town is found in the Etruscan *graffiti* on pottery in several graves.

Excavations at Adria have been hampered by the massive deposits of silt which bury the ancient settlement. Both the wooden foundations of the harbour area and the cemeteries have, however, been located. The earlier graves in the cemeteries were accompanied by a number of imported Attic pots and the presence of several black-figure, as well as later red-figure vessels, would seem to suggest that Adria was founded at a slightly earlier date than Spina. Etruscan products, gold jewellery and bronze statuettes have also been found and, as one might expect, objects from the Este culture, comprising pottery and bronze figurines, are more common here than they were at Spina. During the fourth and third centuries local potters copied classical prototypes; smooth grey-ware kylices and even vessels made in crude imitation of the Apulian red-figure style were manufactured at Adria.

From the fourth century onwards Celtic influence penetrated to Adria. Probably the most remarkable example of this is the chariot burial from the Canal Bianco cemetery. Here, among a group of third-century graves, a two-wheeled chariot was unearthed complete with its two draught horses and a third horse, tethered behind. Iron bits were found in the horses' mouths but unfortunately there were no other objects or even a human burial directly associated.

Plate 67

Although, geographically, Adria seems to be well sited as a port for trade between the Veneti and Greece, it is strange that very few Greek products occur in the main centres of the Este culture. By contrast the role of Spina as an outlet for trade to and from Bologna is clear from the quantities of classical pottery in the Bologna cemeteries.

An ingot of copper, found among the piles of the harbour at Adria, gives us an idea of what may have been exported from Adria, while the fame of the horses bred by the Veneti, recorded by Greek writers, may have been spread by means of a trade in horses through this port.

CISALPINE GAUL

The Greek playwright Aristides of Miletus has left us an entertaining account of how the Celts came to invade Italy. In one of his plays he reveals that the whole invasion was engineered by a certain Aruns, an Etruscan from Chiusi, in order to avenge the seduction of his wife by a fellow-Etruscan. The way he accomplished this was to cross the Alps with waggons laden with wine, oil and figs, and to use these goods to tempt the Celts down into the fertile land of Italy. Although this story cannot be taken too seriously, it does hint at the trade in wine and oil which we know, from archaeological discoveries north of the Alps, was arriving in increasing volume in the halls of the Celtic chieftains in the years just before and after 500 BC. The temptation of the riches of the Po Plain, increased by population pressure at home, must in fact have been a basic reason for the mass migrations from the north.

Although one would expect a more accurate account of events from them, the classical historians contradict one another on the important question of the date of the Celtic invasion of the Po Plain. Livy claimed that this event took place during the reign of the older Tarquin (614–576 BC), when the Insubrian Celts led by Bellovesus entered Northern Italy from across the Western Alps and founded their capital Mediolanum

(Milan) in the Lombard plain; in their wake came the Boii, the Lingones, the Senones and other tribes. Polybius, whose first-hand accounts of Cisalpine Gaul are the most informative as well as the earliest (*c.* 150 BC), by contrast tells us that the Celts did not arrive until about 400 BC, when they came across the Eastern Alps from the Danube basin. Until recently most historians and archaeologists have been content to accept Polybius's account since the first firm historical dates for the presence of the Celts in Italy were the destruction of the Etruscan town of Melpum in about 396 BC and the sack of Rome by Brennus in 390 BC. Now, however, there is some archaeological evidence, as we shall see, to suggest that some groups of Celts were established on the Plain during the fifth century.

To rely on archaeological evidence to solve the problem of when the Celts arrived is no less hazardous than to define their geographical distribution, for the correlation of archaeological assemblages with historical peoples, especially in the case of the Celts in Italy, is a difficult exercise. We see on the one hand that certain Celtic peoples like the Boii, the Lingones and the Senones, who settled near the frontiers of the prosperous native Etruscans and Picenes, adopted Italian fashions so completely that their own La Tène tradition was soon forgotten; on the other hand, in the north-east, we know that other non-Celtic populations like the Veneti and the Raeti were profoundly influenced by Celtic fashions. If we add to this the disagreement among ancient historians as to whether many of the tribes on the periphery were really Celts, indigenous or mixed populations, the limitations of both the archaeological and the historical record are only too evident.

Fig. 78

Although, in view of what we have just said, the geographical and chronological extent of Celtic influence is hazy, the main core of Celtic peoples who settled in the Plain are in fact clearly recognizable as Celts. This group comprised the Insubres in western Lombardy, and the Cenomani between them and the Veneti, while south of the Po, centred on formerly Etruscan Felsina, were the Boii. Beyond the Boii to the east lay the Lingones and, beyond them in the Marche, the Senones, who are geographically outside the scope of this study. Finally we should mention some late arrivals, the Carni, a group of Celts who appeared in the Eastern Alps in 186 BC eclipsing the Santa Lucia culture by settling the Julian Alps near Gorizia.

In the region of the Lombard lakes, and also in Emilia, there appears to be some archaeological evidence for the transition to the Celtic period. As we have seen in chapter VIII the Golasecca territory took on the appearance of a mixed native and Celtic culture by the fourth century without any clear break in continuity being recognizable. All evidence points to a gradual Celtic infiltration of the region and the trans-alpine contacts of the Golasecca I and II periods may in some way anticipate the later spread of Celtic culture. The armaments of the Sesto Calende warriors, the waggon of the Ca' Morta burial and the Golasecca-style pottery of Mont Lassois all show that some kind of liaison existed between Golasecca and Hallstatt as far back as the beginning of the seventh century. There is yet another warrior burial from the Ca' Morta cemetery (grave VIII) dating to the late fifth century that we have not previously mentioned, since this has an even more Celtic appearance than the slightly older Ca' Morta waggon burial. The grave goods from the former include a helmet of the Negau type, which was popular with the Celts both north and south of the Alps, an iron La Tène sword with an anthropomorphic hilt, a spear-head and a Certosa fibula. Bronze La Tène A-style belt plates from the Giubiasco cemetery near Bellinzona (Swiss Ticino) are other objects which had arrived by the end of the fifth century.

The gradual Celticization of the Alpine population during the fourth century BC is further demonstrated by the finds from the cemetery at Cerinasca d'Arbedo, also near Bellinzona. Inhumation burials in the western and central parts of the cemetery were accompanied by grave goods of local Golasecca tradition, while on the eastern side the dead were accompanied by La Tène fibulae, swords and other paraphernelia. Bronze Etruscan flagons of the type traded to the Le Tène chieftains north of the Alps, as well as Golasecca III B pottery were also found in this part of the cemetery. This evidence of the slow infiltration of in-digenous tribes along the alpine fringe of Lombardy does not, however, preclude the likelihood that the Celtic settlement of the Plain was brought about by a massive migration of peoples from across the Alps, people who would be more interested in the fertile plain than the alpine foot-hills.

The earliest Emilian evidence is of a different kind. Here bracelets from Marzabotto and fibulae and belt plates of La Tène A-type from

Bologna and other sites, again suggest an initial penetration by the Celts before the end of the fifth century, although admittedly such objects could have been traded in advance of an invasion.

Of greater interest are a number of fifth-century inhumations in a cemetery at San Martino in Gattara (Ravenna) which, although they have few specifically La Tène elements, do not conform to any local tradition and according to the excavator, Dr Bermond Montanari, possess many features which could be interpreted as Celtic. Here a warrior who had been killed in battle was interred beneath a tumulus with an Etruscan helmet, leg greaves, two spears, iron fire-dogs, bronze situlae and a cauldron, while his garments had been fastened with local fifth-century Certosa and leech brooches. Another tomb contained a one-legged man with an iron crutch, an Attic red-figure pot and an Etruscan beaked flagon, while late-fifth-century pottery came from other graves. At Casola Valsenio (Ravenna) an inhumation was accompanied by silver leech fibulae, a serpentine fibula and an imported Greek black-figure vessel made in Attica between about 480 and 470 BC, as well as a vessel which Professor Hatt has suggested is similar to the French Jogassian Iron Age pottery.

Further west at San Ilario (Reggio Emilia) a cemetery of sixteen inhumations and eight cremations was found in 1878 flanking an old, pre-Roman, metalled roadway. One of the burials was of a man with an iron single-edged short sword and iron bracelet on his right arm and a serpentine iron belt catch. A woman's grave had seven leech fibulae fastening the front of her dress, two fibulae on the shoulders for fastening a cloak and bracelets on both arms with more fibulae clipped to them. Were these fifth-century warriors of Emilia and their womenfolk then Celts, in spite of the absence of typical La Tène or Hallstatt objects, or were they in fact Etruscans, Ligurians or of other local stock? Further research alone can resolve this problem.

If we look at the distribution of Celtic material in Northern Italy, a pattern rather different from that of the earlier Iron Age communities emerges. No longer, especially in Emilia, do we see the large concentrations of population at a few centres but instead a much wider scatter of sites. This, together with the smaller but more numerous burial groups, perhaps reflects a diffuse agricultural society based on small farming communities.

Many new townships or *oppida* were also founded by the Celts, perhaps as markets for the rural population, and a number of the modern cities of the north claim to have a Celtic origin. Among these we find Milan (Mediolanum), Bergamo, Brescia, Cremona, probably Verona, and possibly even Trento. The evidence for these foundations comes mainly from literary sources and only few have produced archaeological evidence of Celtic occupation. La Tène burials have, however, been found at Bologna and Celtic huts and finds at Marzabotto, both of which were former Etruscan centres. Settlement sites on the whole are extremely rare in the archaeological record.

We therefore have to turn, as so often before, to the scattered cemeteries for most of our information about the North Italian Celts. Containing usually not more than a maximum of ten burials these sites contrast with the native Iron Age cemeteries with their hundreds of interments. Only in the north-west, at Ornavasso (Novara) and Bellinzona (Swiss Ticino), do we find large cemeteries containing more than 100 graves but, as we have seen, we may be dealing here, in any case, with a celticized native population.

The distribution map shows how contrasting rites of burial pre-dominated in different parts of the Po Plain. In Lombardy, in the Insubrian territory, inurned cremation was normal, whereas inhumations were found among the Cenomani, the Boii and Lingones. This pattern is not, however, exclusive. In Emilia inhumations are often set in pits lined with pebbles or in stone and brick cists.

Men are frequently accompanied in the grave by weapons. These include the long La Tène iron sword with its iron suspension chain, and the single-edged short sword, a favourite weapon among the Cisalpine Celts which they probably borrowed from the Veneti. One or more spears are normal but the iron throwing spear, or *pilum*, from one of the Bologna graves is exceptional. Fairly common grave goods are the iron shears and iron or bronze strygils. Body armour in the form of Etruscan- or Celtic-type helmets and leg greaves are mostly found south of the Po, where the ideals of Celtic heroism, which shunned the use of armour, were probably moderated by contact with the Etruscans and the Picenes.

Some of the minor Boii chieftains who lived in Bologna, like their Senonian neighbours to the south-east, were buried in a more classical style with funerary wreaths of gold foil leaves on their heads. Glass vessels and even glass gaming sets for entertainment in the after-world were found with other burials at Bologna. In Bologna and in Lombardy, female burials are accompanied by mirrors and a bronze sistrum, a musical instrument of Egyptian origin, was found in a grave at Volongo (Brescia). Personal ornaments are common, especially fibulae, bracelets, neck torques and beads. It is interesting to see that in the San Martino in Gattara tumulus, described earlier, a large *dolium*, probably for holding wine, was found together with a number of cups and other drinking equipment. These as well as the iron fire-dogs and cauldron, found in the same grave, remind one of the idea recently put forward by T. G. E. Powell that the grave goods in the Celtic tombs reflect the obligations of the dead man to his fellow tribesmen, in death as in life, the knight taking his sword to the grave in order to serve his master and the chief his drinking equipment and food for the entertainment of his bondsmen. Finally we can mention the grave of a man accompanied by his horse at Rocca San Casciano (Forli), and a badly disturbed chariot burial also from the San Martino in Gattara cemetery.

The religion of Cisalpine Gaul has left few traces, although evidence of the Celtic practice of head-hunting may be read into Livy's account of the decapitation and ceremonial use of the skull of the Roman proconsul Postumius Albinus, after the defeat of his army near Spina in 216 BC. The cult of sacred wells and pits, sometimes with human sacrifices, which was known all over the Celtic world, has been recognized both at Bologna and Marzabotto where wells containing skeletons dated to the Celtic period of occupation were excavated by Zannoni. In a well in Bologna, a three-foot-high stone interpreted as a cult object was found 30 feet down in the filling; above it lay three bodies which had clearly been thrown into the well.

Celtic metalwork is well represented among grave goods from Northern Italian cemeteries. Iron was used in greater quantity now than ever before for the manufacture of a wide variety of everyday equipment such as weapons, knives, shears, spears, and even helmets. Traces of iron-smelting, probably of Celtic date, have been found stratified between the Etruscan and Roman levels in Bologna.

The bronze-work of this period, by contrast, does not match the high standard and variety that it achieved in earlier times and most of the bronze armour and luxury bronze vessels are imports from Etruria. It is

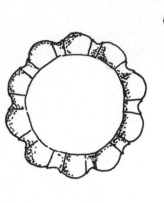

Fig. 79 Manerbio (Brescia). Bronze La Tène bracelet and fragment of hollow silver torque with ram's head and human face

interesting to note that even the characteristic La Tène fibulae do not seem to have been popular south of the Po, where the Certosa and other local Iron Age style fibulae continued to be used.

Silver objects, which by and large are not common in other parts of the Celtic world, have been found in large quantities in Northern Italy. Silver was certainly mined at Eporedia in Val d'Aosta and probably also in the Val Camonica further east, since some of the richest collections of silver come from the provinces of Novara and Brescia immediately adjacent to these deposits. Most of the silver products are of typical La Tène design with fibulae, torques, leg rings and undulating wire bracelets all represented. The most magnificent silver find is the Manerbio hoard (Brescia) which was made up of a series of silver discs varying in diameter embossed with human heads, probably horse *phalerae,* together with a fine hollow silver torque decorated with embossed human and rams' heads. Silver is very common also in the late Celtic Ornavasso cemeteries (Lombardy) during the first century B C when, besides torques and rings, cups were also produced in silver. All but the cups are in La Tène style, the latter probably being produced in nearby Eporedia which had been in Roman control since 100 B C.

Plate 69

Plate 71

Fig. 79

When the Cisalpine Boii were defeated in 199 B C, P. Cornelius Scipio Nasica exhibited as booty in his triumph at Rome 1,500 torques, 247 pounds of gold, and no less than 2,340 pounds of silver.

The Celts appear to have learnt the art of glass working during their stay in the Po Valley, for although the multicoloured glass vessels found in Celtic graves in Bologna were of Mediterranean origin, after 250 B C the Celts started to manufacture their own distinctive coloured glass bracelets somewhere in the Po Valley.

Fig. 81, h

Very little of the pottery found in Celtic graves in the Po Valley resembles the distinctive La Tène pottery found north of the Alps. Only at Pavia and Remedello and some other Lombard cemeteries do we find elegant pottery comparable with the La Tène pottery of Central or Western Europe, although in the region of the Carni to the east there is some characteristic La Tène combed pottery of second-century date.

Fig. 81, a–c

South of the Po the pottery used by the Celts was mostly of a fine grey ware imitating classical-style drinking cups and flagons, while in the second century black glazed Campanian ware of Roman origin became popular. In northern Lombardy it is not really possible to distinguish clearly a Celtic as opposed to a Late Golasecca style of pottery and the situation is further obscured by the adoption of Greek and Roman styles. The forms described for Golasecca III B and C, beakers and 'peg-

Fig. 80

top vessels (*olpe*), are found in graves with pure La Tène metal goods. One of the latter, from a burial at Ardena, has the name '*kasikos*' scratched on the base in the local Lepontian script. A distinctive range of pottery

Fig. 81, d–g

is found in cemeteries of the first century B C like Ornavasso (Novara)

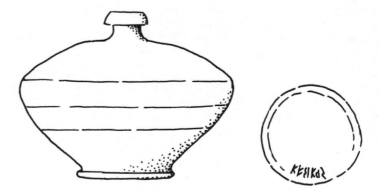

Figs 80, 81 *Above, Peg-top flask (olpe) with 'kasikos' inscription from Ardena (Como). Right, Pottery used by the Celts in Northern Italy. a–c Bologna, third and fourth century; d–g Ornavasso-San Bernardino (Novara), first century* B C; *h Remedello*

and Pavia. In these are found small pots with over-all rusticated decoration, done with finger-nail impression, and butt beakers with splayed
rims and criss-cross incised decoration over the body. Angular Roman
flagons are also common in these graves.

This great variety of pottery style in the Po Valley is a good object
lesson in the dangers and difficulties of trying to correlate pottery styles
and population groups during a period when there was considerable
foreign influence and also extensive trade in mass-produced pottery.

For evidence of the economy of the Celts we must turn to contemporary
literary sources. Polybius in the second century B C in one passage describes the fertile fields of the Celts of the Po Plain growing with an
abundance of wheat, barley, millet, and vines and stocked with pigs.
However, he elsewhere contradicts this observation by saying that the
North Italian Celts led a simple life in which warfare and pastoralism
featured largely, and wealth was measured in gold and flocks.

At the end of the third century B C the Celts living north of the Po
started to produce their own coinage, significantly enough in silver,
based on the drachma of Marseilles. Most of these coins are found in the
lands of the Insubres, Lepontii and Cenomani north of the Po, for by

this time Emilia was under Roman control, Roman coinage being introduced through the colonies of Cremona and Piacenza and Bologna. Some of the coins of northern Lombardy are inscribed with legends in the Lepontian alphabet.

A large hoard composed entirely of North Italian drachmas has been found as far afield as Cornwall in the British Isles – one would like to think of it as a payment for a consignment of Cornish tin for the North Italian market.

ROMAN EPILOGUE

Slowly but surely Northern Italy came under the power of Rome, a process which took more than two hundred years to complete. After the defeat of the Celts at Telamon in Etruria in 225 BC the Roman armies pressed home their victory by entering the homeland of the Celts, and for the first time crossed into the Po Plain. This first intrusion involved a rapid campaign over a wide area of the central Po Plain as far as the Insubrian *oppidum* of Mediolanum (Milan), which was destroyed. Shortly afterwards the first colonies and trading posts were established among the Cisalpine Celts at Placentia (Piacenza) and Cremona in 219 BC.

After the interval caused by the Second Punic War a series of long-drawn-out conflicts took place. The Boii in Emilia put up a tenacious resistance but were finally vanquished in 191 BC. At the end of this campaign, according to Strabo, Scipio reported that only the very old and children were left alive, and the remainder were expelled from Italy. A different account is given by Livy, however, for he wrote that the Boii only had to give up half their lands and cede Bologna in return for peace. A Latin colony was founded at Bononia (Bologna) in 189 and Roman colonies at Mutina (Modena) and Parma in 188 BC. Aquileia to the north-east was founded as a base for operations in Eastern Europe in 181 BC and the Veneti came into the Roman fold in 182 BC.

Although Marcellus penetrated deep into Lombardy and defeated the Insubres and their allies the Orobi, at Como in 196 BC, the territories to the north of the Po, apart from the Veneto, remained largely under Celtic control until well into the first century.

A further stage in the conquest of the north involved the subjugation of the mountain tribes. In the north-west the celticized mountain people known as the Salassi, in the Val d'Aosta, were from an early date of interest to the Romans since they controlled not only the Great St Bernard Pass but also important gold and silver deposits. The Romans took over the mining areas in Salassian territory in 143 BC and their armies were allowed to cross the Great St Bernard through Salassian territory on payment of one drachma for each soldier. This co-operation lasted until 25 BC when, following the plunder of an army pay chest, the Romans subdued the tribe by force of arms and sold the whole population of 44,000 people into slavery.

The final conquest of the Alpine valleys occurred in 15 BC under Drusus and the effect of these campaigns is reflected in the destruction of several of the hill-forts we examined in chapter VIII, as well as in the impoverishment of the La Tène cemeteries at Ornavasso. Of the two Ornavasso cemeteries, called San Bernadino and Persona, the former has rich grave goods and clearly ante-dates the Roman attack, while the poor-quality finds from the latter and the more direct Roman influence post-dates the event.

There is little evidence of Celtic or other native elements surviving Romanization for long, in either the literary or the archaeological record. Celtic religion persisted in some areas as we can see from dedications to the three Matronae and Belenus, another Celtic deity. The presence of Celtic names on tombstones of the Roman period in Emilia indicates survival of local tradition here, and incidentally supports Livy's, as against Strabo's, account of the defeat of the Boii.

Only in the Alps can we recognize a much longer survival of pre-historic elements into the Roman period. The names of the Raetian tribes indeed have remained with us till the present day, fossilized in the names of the valleys which they once inhabited. Thus we find in Val di Non, north-west of Trento, the home of the Anauni; the Camuni in the Val Camonica; the Isarci in the Eisack or Isarco valley, and the Sabini in the Val Sabbia; similar names are preserved in other parts of the Alps. It is the same with the archaeological remains, too, for in the Central Alps La Tène style fibulae, and the flagon with a single long handle and flattened side, derived from flagons used in the San Zeno period and ultimately from the jugs of Melaun, survived for much of the Roman period.

Bibliography

GENERAL WORKS

MONTELIUS, O. *La Civilisation Primitive en Italie*, Stockholm 1895–1910.

PEET, T. E. *The Stone and Bronze Ages in Italy*, Oxford 1909.

PITTIONI, R. *Italien, Urgeschichtliche Kulturen* (Real-Encyclopädie der Classichen Altertumswissenschaft; A. Pauly, G. Wissowa and W. Kroll), Stuttgart 1962.

RADMILLI, A. M. (ed.) *Piccola Guida della Preistoria Italiana*, Florence 1962
— *La Preistoria d'Italia alla luce delle ultime scoperte*, Florence, 1963.

WALKER, D. S. *A Geography of Italy*, London 1958.

REGIONAL STUDIES

CANNARELLA, D. *Il carso e la sua preistoria*, Trieste 1959.

ISSEL, A. *Liguria Preistorica*, Genoa 1901.

LEONARDI, P. *Preistoria Vicentina, Studi in onore di Federigo M. Mistorigo*, Vicenza 1958.

MANSUELLI, G. A. and SCARANI, R. *Emilia prima dei Romani*, Milan 1961.

SCRANI, R. Repertorio di Scavi e Scoperte dell'Emilia e Romagna, *Preistoria dell' Emilia e Romagna*, vol. II, Bologna 1963.

PITTIONI, R. *Stand und Aufgabe der Urgeschichtlichen Forschung im Oberetsch*, Bolzano 1940.

PALAEOLITHIC AND MESOLITHIC

LEONARDI, P. and BROGLIO, A. Ricerche sul Paleolitico Emiliano, *Preistoria dell'Emilia e Romagna*, vol. I, Bologna 1962.
— Le Paléolithique de la Vénétie, *Annali dell'*

Università di Ferrara. Sez. XV. (Supplement to vol. I), 1962.

BROGLIO, A. Le industrie mousteriane della Grotta del Broion, *Memorie del Museo Civico di Storia Naturale di Verona*, vol. XII 1964.
— Il riparo 'Raffaello Battaglia' presso Asiago, *Rivista di Scienze Preistoriche*, vol. XIX 1964.

CARDINI, L. Gli Strati Paleolitici e Mesolitici delle Arene Candide, *Rivista di Studi Liguri*. XII 1946.

CANNARELLA, D. and CREMONESI, G. Gli Scavi nella Grotta Azzurra di Samartorza, *Rivista di Scienze Preistoriche*, vol. XXII 1967.

NEOLITHIC

BARFIELD, L. Scavi sulla Rocca di Rivoli 1963, *Memorie del Museo Civico di Storia Naturale di Verona*, vol. XIV 1966.

BARFIELD, L. and BROGLIO, A. Nuove Osservazioni sull' Industria de Le Basse di Valcalaona, *Rivista di Scienze Preistoriche*, vol. XX 1965.
— Materiali per lo studio del Neolitico del Territorio Vicentino, *Bullettino di Paletnologia Italiana*, vol. 75 1966.

BAROCELLI, P. Sepolcreti Neolitici dell'Italia Occidentale, *Bolletino della Società Piemontese di Archeologia*, vol. VII 1923.

BERNABÒ BREA, L. *Gli Scavi nella Caverna delle Arene Candide*, vol. I 1946, vol. II 1956, Bordighera.

GUERRESCHI, G. *La Lagozza di Besnate*, Como 1967.

KOROŠEC, J. Neolit na Krasu in v Slovenskem Primorju, *Zgodovinski Casopis,* vol. 14 1960.

MALAVOLTI, F. *Appunti per una cronologia relativa del Neo-Eneolitico Emiliano* Emilia Preromana, vols. 2, 3 1951–52.

MARCHESETTI, C. Ricerche preistoriche nelle Caverne di San Canziano presso Trieste, *Bolletino della Società Adriatica di Scienze Naturali di Trieste,* 1889.

ZORZI, F. I Vasi a Bocca Quadrata dei Livelli Superiori del Deposito Quarternario di Quinzano Veronese. '*In Memorie di Fernando Malavolti*', Modena 1956.

COPPER AGE

COLINI, G. A. Il Sepolcreto di Remedello Sotto nel Bresciano ed il Periodo Eneolitico in Italia. Serialized article in the *Bullettino di Paletnologia Italiana* between the years 1898 and 1902.

CROWFOOT, J. W. Note on excavations in a Ligurian Cave, 1907–1909, *Man* 1926.

GHISLANZONI, E. La Tomba Eneolitica di Villafranca Veronese, *Bullettino di Paletnologia Italiana,* 1939.

ZORZI, F. Resti di un Abitato Capannicolo Eneolitico alle Colombare di Negrar, *Actes du IV Congrés International du Quarternaire* 1953.

ROCK ART

ANATI, E. *The Camonica Valley,* New York 1961.

— *Arte Preistorica in Valtellina,* Capo di Ponte 1968.

BICKNELL, C. *A Guide to the Prehistoric Rock Engravings in the Maritime Alps,* Bordighera 1913.

ORNELLA ACANFORA, M. Le Statue Antropomorfe dell'Alto Adige, *Cultura Atesina,* VI 1952–55.

EARLY BRONZE AGE

BATTAGLIA, R. La Palafitta del Lago di Ledro nel Trentino, *Memorie del Museo di Storia Naturale di Trento,* vol. 7 1943.

FERRARI, M. and TOMASI, G. *La Valle di Ledro e le Palafitte,* Rovereto 1969.

MUNRO, R. *The Lake Dwellings of Europe,* London 1890.

SCARABELLI, G. Stazione Preistorica sul Monte Castellaccio presso Imola, Imola 1887.

SCARANI, R. Gli Scavi nella Tanaccia di Brisighella, *Preistoria dell'Emilia e Romagna,* vol. II 1963.

ZORZI, F. La Palafitta di Barche di Solferino, *Bullettino di Paletnologia Italiana,* 1940.

MIDDLE AND LATE BRONZE AGE

ASPES, A. and FASANI, L. La Stazione Preistorica di Bor di Pacengo e la Media Età del Bronzo nel anfiteatro morenico del Garda, *Atti e Memorie dell'Accademia di Agricoltura Scienze a Lettere di Verona,* 1967–68.

COWEN, J. D. The Origins of the Flange-hilted Sword of Bronze in Continental Europe, *Proceedings of the Prehistoric Society,* vol. XXXII 1966.

PERONI, R. L'Età del Bronzo Medio e Recente tra l'Adige e il Mincio, *Memorie del Museo Civico di Storia Naturale di Verona,* vol. XI 1963.

RITTATORE VONWILLER, F. La Necropoli di Canegrate. *Sibrium* vol. I 1953–54, vol. III 1956–57.

SÄFLUND, G. *Le Terremare delle Provincie di Modena, Reggio Emilia Parma e Piacenza,* Lund 1939.

PROTO-VILLANOVAN AND
FINAL BRONZE AGE

ASPES, A., BELLINTANI, G. F. and FASANI, L.
*I materiali della stazione proto-veneta di Villa-
marzana (Rovigo)*, Padusa VI 1970.

MÜLLER KARPE, H. *Beiträge zur Chronologie
der Urnenfelderzeit Nordlich und Sudlich der
Alpen*, Berlin 1959.

SCHUHMACHER, E. *Die Proto-villanova Fund-
gruppe*, Bonn 1967.

IRON AGE BOLOGNA AND THE
ETRUSCANS

DUCATI, P. Le Pietre Funerarie Felsinee,
Monumenti Antichi, vol. XX, 1911.

MANSUELLI, G. A. Struttura ed Economia di
Bologna Villanoviana, '*Civiltà del Ferro*',
Bologna 1960.

RANDALL MACIVER, D. *Villanovans and
Early Etruscans*, Oxford 1924.

SCULLARD, H. H. *The Etruscan Cities and Rome*,
London 1967.

ZANNONI, A. *Gli Scavi della Certosa di Bologna*,
Bologna 1876.

ESTE, GOLASECCA AND LIGURIA

FREY, O. H. *Die Entstehung der Situlenkunst*,
Berlin 1969.

RANDALL MACIVER, D. *The Iron Age in Italy*,
Oxford 1927.

SOPRINTENDENZA ALLE ANTICHITA DELLE
VENEZIE, *Arte e Civiltà dei Veneti Antichi*,
Padua 1968.

MARCHESETTI, C. *I Castellieri Preistorici di
Trieste e della Regione Giulia*, Trieste 1903.

CRIVELLI, A. La Necropoli di Ascona.
Sibrium, vol. I 1953–54.

RITTATORE VONWILLER, F. *La Necropoli
Preromana della Ca'Morta*, Como 1966.

KOSSAK, G. Zur den Metallbeigaben des
Wagengrabes von Ca'Morta, *Sibrium*, vol.
III 1956–57.

LAMBOGLIA, N. La Necropoli Ligure di
Chiavari, *Rivista di Studi Liguri*, XXVI
1960.

VON MERHARDT, G. Archäologisches zur
Frage der Illyrer in Tyrol, *Wiener Prä-
historische Zeitschrift*, 14, 1927.

FOGOLARI, G. San Zeno nella Anaunia,
'*Civiltà del Ferro*', Bologna 1960.

SPINA, ADRIA AND THE CELTS

ALFIERI, N. Spina e le nuove scoperte. Prob-
lemi Archeologici e Urbanistici, *Atti del
Io Convegno di Studi Etruschi*, Florence
1959.

FORLATI TAMARO, B. Il Problema di Adria,
Atti del Io Convegno di Studi Etruschi, 1959.

BRIZIO, E. Le Necropoli Galliche della
Provincia di Bologna, *Atti e Memorie della
Romagna*, 1887.

LAVIOSA ZAMBOTTI, P. L'Invasione Gallica
in Val Padana, *Storia di Milano*, vol. I,
Milan 1953.

REINACH, S. and BERTRAND, M. *Les Celtes et
les Gaulois dans la Vallée du Po et du Danube*,
Paris 1894.

PAUTASSO, A. Le Monete Preromane dell'
Italia Settentrionale, *Sibrium*, vol. VII
1962–63.

SOURCES OF THE PLATES

Photographs taken by the author include plates 7, 9, 10, 11, 12, 13, 15, 16, 17, 18, 21, 22, 25, 26, 39, 40, 47, 63, 72. The other photographs were kindly supplied by the following people and institutions: Direzione delle Belle Arti del Comune di Genoa 1, 19; Professor A. Broglio (Ferrara) 4, 14; Professor P. Graziosi (Florence) 3; Museo Civico di Storia Naturale di Verona 5; Professor L. Cardini (Rome) 6; Museo Civico Archeologico Bologna 8, 42, 43–45; Tapparo e Trentin, Vicenza 20; Museo Romano, Brescia 69, 71; Soprintendenza alle Antichità, Padua 23, 24, 41, 48–53; Ashmolean Museum, Oxford, 27; Museo Trentino di Storia Naturale, Trento 30, 31, 33; E. Quiresi (Cremona) 32, 57–59, 67, 68; Museo Civico, Gavardo 35, 36; Museo Nazionale di Antichità, Parma 37, 38, 46, 70; Professor N. Lamboglia 64, 65; Dr R. Perini (Trento) 66; Dr V. Valvassori (Ferrara) 73; Professor Rittattore Vonwiller (Milan) 61, 62; Museo Civico, Como 60; Musée de l'Homme (Paris) 2; Dr E. Anati (Capo di Ponte) 28, 29. Plates 54–56 are taken from Kastelic, *Situla Art;* Plate 34 is taken from R. Battaglia's La Palafitta del Lago di Ledro nel Trentino: *Memorie del Museo Civico di Storia Naturale della Venezia Tridentina,* vol. VII 1943 pl. VIII 2.

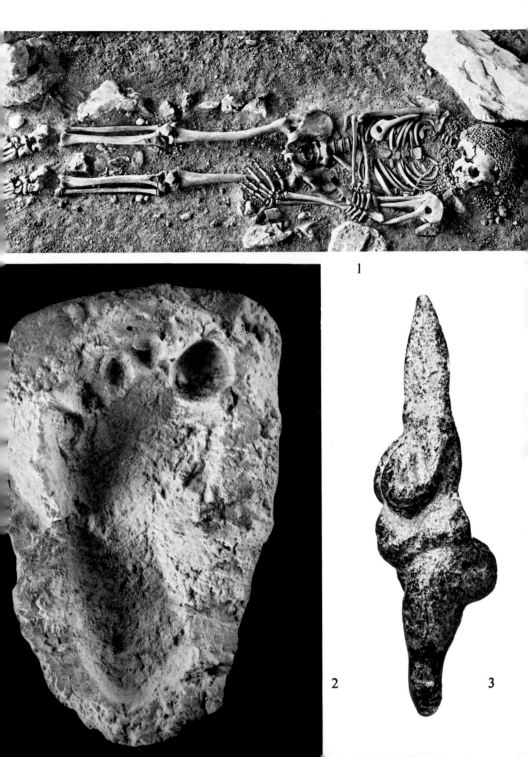

1

2

3

4

5

6

7

8 9

10 11

12

13, 14

15, 16

17

19

18

20

21

22

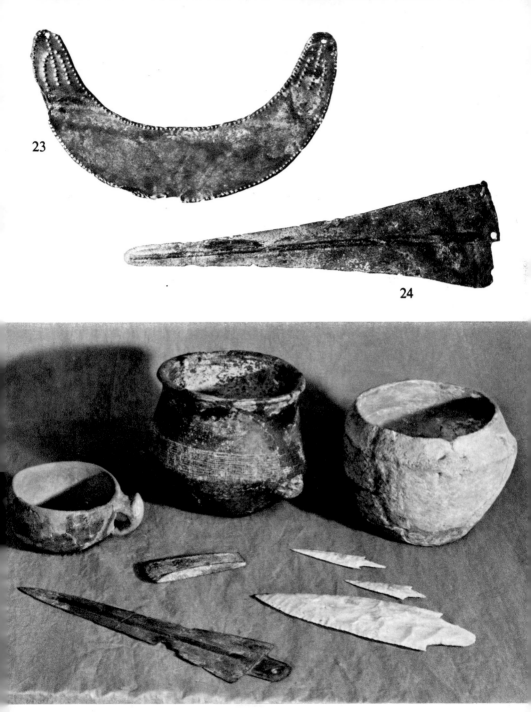

23

24

25

26

27

28, 29

32

33

34

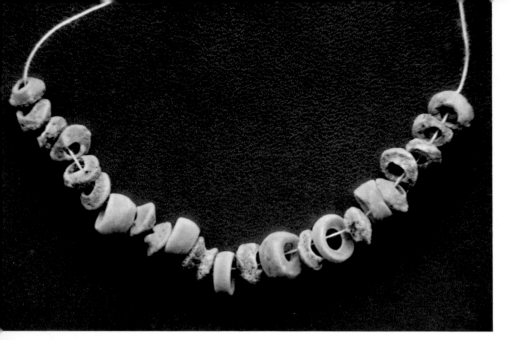

35

36

37

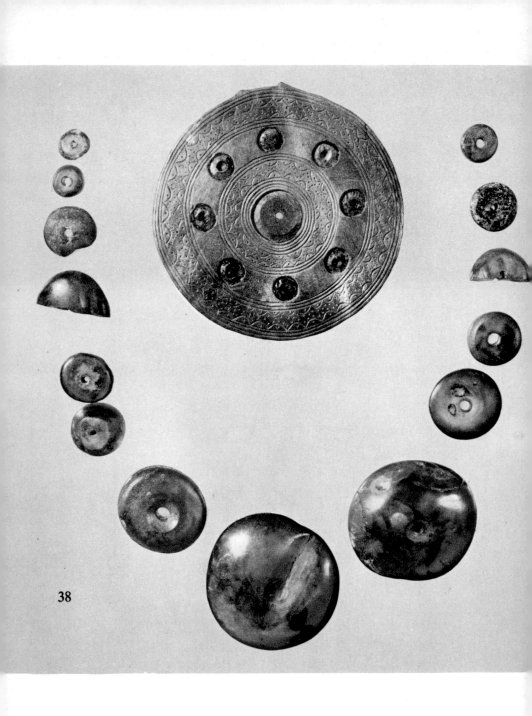

38

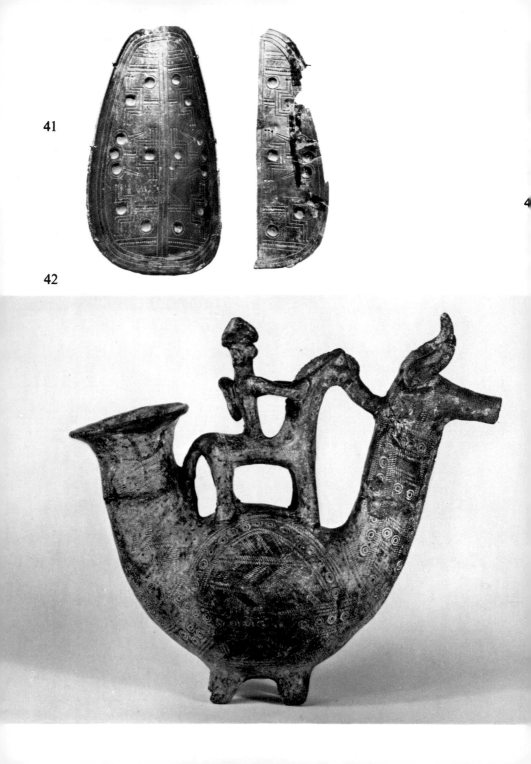

41

42

44, 45

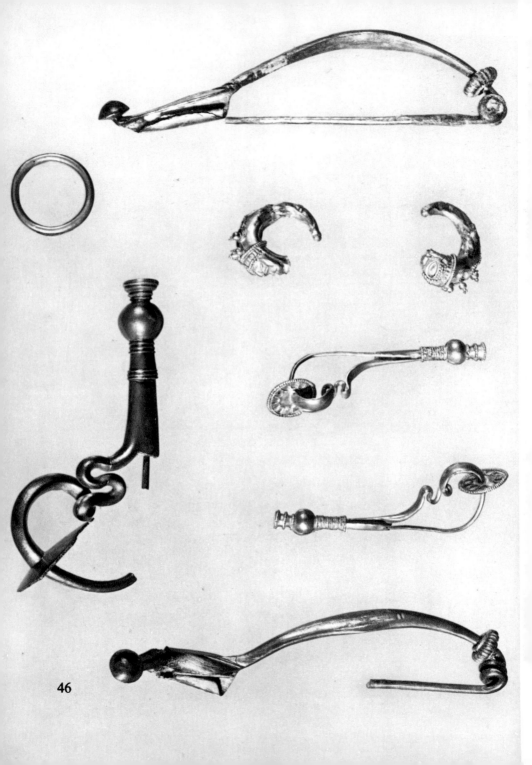

46

47

48, 49

51

52

53

54

55

56

57

58

60

59

61, 62

63

64

65

66

67

68

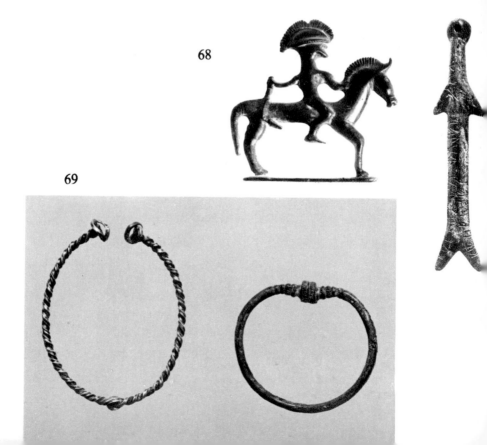

69

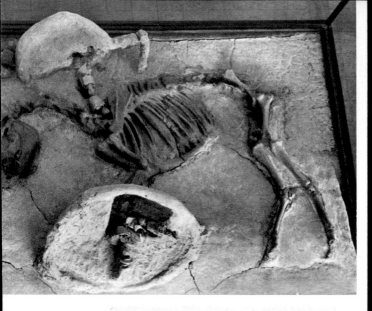

71

70

Notes on the Plates

1 An Epi-Gravettian burial dating from the final stages of the Wurm glaciation found in the cave of Arene Candide (Finale). The young man had been buried with four perforated 'batons de commandements', a rib knife, a pendant and a shell-ornamented cap. The photograph is of the reconstructed burial now in the Museo Civico di Archeologia Ligure at Pegli.

2 Impression of the foot print of a Neanderthal man from the Grotta della Basura, at Toirano (Liguria). 21.1 cm. long. (Musée de l'Homme, Paris).

3 Gravettian style mother goddess figurine found at Savignano (Modena). Made of serpentine and 22 cm. high, this is one of the largest Gravettian figurines known. It is also inexplicably the only Upper Palaeolithic find from Emilia. (Museo Pigorini, Rome).

4 View of the rock shelter Riparo Tagliente in the Valpantena north of Verona. This site was occupied at the end of the Pleistocene period by Final Epi-Gravettian hunters. The shelter can be seen at the foot of the white limestone cliff in the centre of the photograph.

5 The natural limestone bridge known as the Ponte di Veia in the Lessini Mountains north of Verona. Formed by the collapse of the inner roof of a large cave, the site was a focal point for Palaeolithic and later pre-

historic settlement. The view shown here looks down through the former entrance of the cave. Stratified Palaeolithic remains have been found in the smaller cave to the left of the bridge where the tent belonging to the excavation team directed by Pasa and Zorzi is pitched.

6 An extended burial from the cemetery in the Mesolithic levels of the cave of Arene Candide (Finale). The body is that of a child with a necklace or cape of squirrels' tails on its chest and shells and pebbles near its head.

7 Wooden platform constructed by the makers of the early style of square-mouthed pottery (Quinzano-Finale stage), on the shores of Lake Fimon at Molino Casarotto (Vicenza). The criss-crossed wooden timbers of the platform run into a large stone hearth.

8 Ring of jade with a triangular cross-section from the province of Bologna. These rings may have been bracelets or were possibly fixed round the head of a mace. They have been found in association with Fiorano and Square-Mouthed Pottery Culture assemblages, frequently of material other than jade. The jade probably came from Piedmont or eastern Liguria. Outer diameter 10 cm. (Museo Civico Archeologico, Bologna).

9 Jade axe from the province of Reggio Emilia. This is a fine example of the large

'ceremonial' jade axes which were being traded throughout Western Europe during the Neolithic period and which are found as far north as the British Isles. The source of these axes may well have been Piedmont. Length 21 cm. (Musei Civici di Reggio Emilia).

10 Large cooking pot with four handles and vertical ribbed decoration from a pit containing material of the Fiorano Culture at Chiozza, a site which is better known for its Square-Mouthed Pottery Culture settlement. Height 26 cm. (Musei Civici di Reggio Emilia).

11 Arrow found preserved in peat at Molino Casarotto (Vicenza). The shaft is of wood and the tanged flint tip was attached by means of a fine clay 'putty' bound with twine. Found at the edge of a Square-Mouthed Pottery Culture platform in 1970. Length: 28 cm.

12 Profile of a hearth of stone and clay which had been rebuilt some six times at Molino Casarotto (Vicenza). Alternating levels of mussel shell (white) and carbonized water chestnut husks (black) can be seen at the base of the section.

13 Plain square-mouthed beaker from Molino Casarotto (Vicenza) Height: 11 cm.

14 Square-mouthed beaker with scratched designs from San Germano, a settlement of the early Square-Mouthed Pottery Culture in a peat basin a few miles to the south of Molino Casarotto. Height: 18 cm. (Museo di Vicenza).

15 The naturally defended settlement on the Rocca di Rivoli (Verona) which dominates the northern end of the Adige gorge and the route to the Central Alpine passes. Occupied initially during the two later stages of the Square-Mouthed Pottery Culture, it was re-settled in the Early Bronze Age, the Final Bronze Age and again in post-Roman times.

16 Circular pits, probably for storage, excavated in 1966 on the Rocca di Rivoli (Verona). These date to the Rivoli-Castelnovo stage of the Square-Mouthed Pottery Culture. Scale is one metre.

17 Fragments of pottery decorated with incised and cut-out motifs which include spiral and straight line geometric patterns from the Chiozza—Rivoli 'Spiazzo' stage of occupation on the Rocca di Rivoli (Verona). (Museo Civico di Storia Naturale, Verona).

18 Clay figurine with shoulder length hair and hands against the chest, from the Rivoli-Castelnovo stage of occupation of the Rocca di Rivoli (Verona).

19 A group of four ornamental clay stamps (pintaderas) from Arene Candide (Liguria). These are characteristic objects of the Square-Mouthed Pottery Culture and were probably used for ornamenting the body. The two in the top row have a flat decorated surface and a grip at the back; the two lower examples are unusual in being cylindrical with a perforation through the centre. (Museo Civico di Archeologia Ligure, Pegli).

20 Bowl decorated with hatched pendent triangles of the type used on settlements of the Rivoli‑Castelnovo stage of the Square‑Mouthed Pottery Culture in the Veneto. This example was found in the cave of Bocca Lorenza in mountains to the north of Vicenza.

21 The promontory settlement at Pescale (Modena). This site, overlooking the Sec‑chia River, is in a similar position to the Rocca di Rivoli and was also occupied during the later stages of the Neolithic.

22 The cave of Orso di Gabrovizza (Trieste) carved out of the Karst limestone. It was used as a shelter by Late Neolithic popu‑lations. Similar caves in the area show evi‑dence of occupation mainly during the period between the Palaeolithic and Early Bronze Age.

23 Silver chest‑ornament or pectoral with em‑bossed dot decoration from the Copper Age grave at Villafranca Veronese. This is one of the few silver objects known from Europe during the third millennium. Overall width about 30 cm. (Soprintendenza alle Antich‑ità, Padua).

24 Copper halberd from the burial at Villa‑franca Veronese. The Italians of the third millennium appear to have adapted the straight heeled dagger blades of East Mediterranean origin to be used as halberds. That it was in fact a halberd and not a dagger can be seen in the slight asymmetry in the angle between mid‑rib and the line of the rivet holes. Length 36.2 cm. (Soprinten‑denza alle Antichità, Padua).

25 Pottery, copper and flint grave‑goods from the Copper Age cemetery of Remedello di Sotto (Brescia). These objects reflect some of the varied external influences that contri‑buted to the development of the Remedello tradition. The elbow handle on the pot on the left is of South Italian inspiration, the metope design on the centre bowl suggests contacts with the Fontbouïsse culture of southern France and the tanged copper blade has Aegean and Anatolian prototypes. (Musei Civici di Reggio Emilia).

26 Pottery from the Beaker Culture grave at Ca' di Marco (Brescia). Two bell beakers of the 'international' zoned type on the left were here associated with a black strap‑handled cup which has clear parallels in Central Europe. (Musei Civici di Reggio Emilia).

27 Grave‑goods found with collective burials in the small cave of Tana Bertrand (Liguria). The re‑strung necklace is composed of marble and steatite beads. The beads are mostly of the simple cylindrical type but 'single drop' and winged types are also re‑presented. Enclosed by the necklace are a pendant made from a fragment of boar's tusk and a flint arrow‑head. (Ashmolean Museum, Oxford).

28 Statue menhir from Paspardo, Val Camon‑ica, showing collar, 'belt', weapons and a stag.

29 Rock surface at Capo di Ponte, Val Camonica, covered with representations of fields and houses.

30 View of the Early Bronze Age lake‑side

settlement of Molina di Ledro (Trento) shortly after its discovery. Note the original height of the water before the lake was drained at the reed line in the background.

31 Horizontal plank flooring in the Early Bronze Age settlement of Molina di Ledro. This photo was again taken during Battaglia's excavations on the site.

32 Two-handled pot with characteristic elbow handles of Polada type from the settlement at Molina di Ledro. Plastic decoration of this sort is also a common feature of Polada pottery. (Museo Nazionale Trentino, Trento).

33 Wooden piles and horizontal cross ties found during Battaglia's excavations at Molina di Ledro (1927–37).

34 Crook ard found preserved among the piles of the settlement at Molina di Ledro during Battaglia's excavations.

35 A collection of beads found together in the Early Bronze Age settlement of Lucone di Polpenazzo (Brescia). The biconical beads, one of which is segmented, are of a glassy frit, (faïence) while the smooth white ones are of marble (Museo Civico di Gavardo).

36 Lucone di Polpenazzo (Brescia). Dug-out canoe carved from a trunk of oak found in the Early Bronze Age Polada settlement. With its well-carved prow (detail) it is a good example of many such prehistoric canoes that have been found in the peat beds and lakes of Northern Italy. A cast of this canoe is now exhibited in the Museo Civico di Gavardo.

37 Five daggers of Early Bronze Age date from the hoard of Castione dei Marchesi (Parma). This find was made about a quarter of a mile from the famous Middle and Late Bronze Age Terremare site of the same name. The solid hilts, the ogival openings on the hilt plates and the linear engraving on these weapons clearly betray their relationship with the contemporary dagger traditions of the Unêtice and other cultures of the area to the north of the Alps. (Museo Nazionale di Antichità, Parma).

38 Incised bone disc and amber beads from the terramara of Castione dei Marchesi (Parma). The large disc has a series of recessed circles some of which still retained traces of adhesive resin. It was probably originally inlaid with amber. The disc is 9.5 cm. in diameter. (Museo Nazionale di Antichità).

39 Fine and coarse ware pottery from different Terremare settlements in the province of Reggio Emilia. (Musei Civici di Reggio Emilia).

40 Urns and other grave goods from the Proto-Villanovan cemetery of Bismantova (Reggio Emilia). Note the characteristic out-turned rims of the urns and their equally distinctive grooved shoulders and dot bordered linear decoration. The arc fibula is the 'type fossil' of this phase but the lunate razor shown on this plate is more at home in the context of the ensuing initial stage of the Iron Age in nearby Bologna. (Musei Civici di Reggio Emilia).

41 Bronze shin guards with repoussée decoration from Pergine (Trento). Although the

embossed design incorporating the sun boat and swan motif has a long life in Italy the early style of these pieces dates them to the Proto-Villanovan period.

42 Pottery vessel in the shape of a horned beast with a horse and rider on its back from the Benacci cemetery at Bologna. It is uncertain whether this pot should be described as 'ritual', a toy or just purely decorative. Note the technique of false cord decoration which was first introduced to the north in Proto-Villanovan times. (Museo Civico Archeologico, Bologna).

43 Grave stone with a stylised anthropomorphic outline, carved in shallow relief with an orientalizing design of sphinxes and the Tree of life. Found at the Saletta di Bentivoglio in Bologna, this stele dates to the sixth century B C. (Museo Civico Archeologico, Bologna).

44, 45 Pedestalled bowls with bosses, pendent chain and incised and impressed decoration found in the Stradello Certosa cemetery in Bologna and probably of seventh century date. (Museo Civico Archeologico, Bologna).

46 Gold objects from an Etruscan tomb at Fraore (Parma) dating to the fifth century. They comprise a pair of Certosa fibulae, serpentine fibulae with characteristically late features of the ball foot and stop disc, earrings with masks and granular decoration and a small ring. (Museo Nazionale di Antichità, Parma).

47 Clay statuette found with 'Etruscan' inhumation burials at Remedello di Sotto (Brescia). The same burials contained Etruscan bucchero pottery. (Musei Civici, Reggio Emilia).

48 Urn from the Este I cemetery on the shores of Lake Garda at Garda (Verona). The squat form and the grooved decoration are still very much in the preceding Proto-Villanovan tradition. (Soprintendenza alle Antichità, Padua).

49 Urn decorated in the false cord technique from grave 131 in the Casa di Ricovero cemetery at Este. It dates to Este period II. (Museo Archeologico, Este).

50 Bird vessel on wheels from grave no. 2 in the Pelà cemetery at Este. This object dates from period I at Este and could possibly be a child's toy although the bird appears to have religious overtones as well. Note the false cord decoration which is similar to that on the animal pot from Bologna (Plate 42). (Museo Archeologico, Este).

51 Situlate pottery urn from grave 58 in the Benvenuti cemetery at Este. The decoration is done with applied bronze studs and is clearly an imitation of the repoussée designs on the more expensive bronze Kurd situlae. Transitional Este II to III phase, early sixth century. (Museo Archeologico, Este).

52 Urn of the Este III period with a fitting cup lid and black and red zoned decoration. Found at Este. (Museo Archeologico, Este).

53 Beaker in the shape of a boot from the Nazari cemetery Este. Dating to Este period III. (Museo Archeologico, Este).

54 A detail of the Certosa situla showing a musical contest between two players sitting on a settee decorated with ducks and orientalizing beasts. (Museo Civico, Bologna).

55 Another detail from the Certosa situla, showing the head of one of the warriors who is wearing a helmet probably made of leather with metal discs sewn to it. The large nose and bulbous cheeks are a characteristic feature of the human heads represented in situla art.

56 The Certosa situla from Bologna. Here one can see the zonal arrangement of the decoration with a procession of soldiers in the upper register, preparations for a feast in the second, scenes of rural life and entertainment in the third and exotic beasts borrowed from Corinthian pottery in the lower register.

57 Warrior figure with shield, spear and crested helmet found in a cemetery on the Lozzo canal at Este. The helmet is like the crested ones in fashion in Italy before the seventh century, but the figure is of a more recent date. (Museo Archeologico, Este).

58 Bronze figurine of a woman in local Venetic costume, found in the votive deposit at Caldevigo, Este. Este period IV. (Museo Archeologico, Este).

59 Bronze horseman found in a votive hoard dedicated to the goddess Reitia, at Este. The spear is a replacement. (Museo Archeologico, Este).

60 Four wheeled waggon with iron tyres and bronze sheathed hubs, spokes, chassis and balustrade. This vehicle was found in the Ca'Morta cemetery associated with grave goods dating to the mid fifth century BC. The type of waggon is very like those buried with the nobility of the Late Hallstatt culture in eastern France and southern Germany, at the end of the sixth century. (Museo Civico, Como).

61 Duck-shaped vessel of Golasecca II date from the Iron Age cemetery of Ca'Morta (Como). Bird vessels are a recurrent type in the Iron Age in both Italy and Central Europe. (Museo Civico, Como).

62 Double incense bowl, detachable from the stand. Resin found adhering to these vessels suggests their use as incense burners. The decoration of stamped rosettes is rare on Golasecca ceramics and shows the influence of the Emilian Arnoaldi pottery. Late Golasecca II. (Museo Civico, Como).

63 Stone rampart on the Iron Age 'Castelliere' of Monte San Leonardo (Trieste), seen from the outside. This is one of the several hundred fortifications crowning the limestone hills of the Karst regions of Trieste and Istria.

64 View of the eighth century cremation cemetery at Chiavari (Liguria). Individual and 'family' burials are enclosed by circular and rectangular slab built fences.

65 Rectangular stone built houses in the hillfort of the Ligurian Iron Age on Monte Bignone (San Remo).

66 Rectangular cellared house of the San Zeno period at Montesei di Serso (Trento) This

lower floor level has a double ramp entrance and a central dividing wall.

67 Chariot with two draught-horses and charger found in the third century cemetery of Canal Bianco at Adria. The chariot burial may represent Celtic influence in this busy international port. (Museo Civico, Adria).

68 Bronze objects from the large votive deposit found in the village of San Zeno (Trento). Right, pendents in the shape of highly stylised male and female figures, both inscribed with the local Iron Age script. Left, mounted warrior wearing a Celtic helmet. (Museo Nazionale Trentino, Trento).

69 A two part silver wire torque found in a Celtic burial at Remedello in 1886, and a bronze torque with decorated seal ends from a Celtic grave found at Carpendolo in 1897. Both from the Museo Romano, Brescia.

70 Caselvatica (Parma). Bronze helmet with scalloped cheek pieces from a La Tène burial. The thin embossed sheet-bronze

horn attachments were added at a later date. (Museo Nazionale di Antichità, Parma).

71 Silver discs, probably horse ornaments, from the hoard of silver objects found at Manerbio (Brescia). The severed head motif was a popular one with the La Tène metal workers. (Museo Romano, Brescia).

72 Engravings on the ice-polished surfaces of the slopes of Monte Baldo at Punta San Virgilio overlooking Lake Garda. The ships shown include a paddle steamer of the nineteenth century AD. Other nearby engravings studied by Professor Pasotti appear to be Iron Age in date.

73 Aerial photograph of the ancient canal system in the port of Spina (Ferrara). The broad dark band running across the bottom of the picture is the silted arm of the River Po. The main arterial canal in the town runs across the top left hand corner while to the right of this lies the network of canals belonging to the main settlement area. Photograph taken by Valvassori in 1956.

Index

Index

Index